75 YEARS

VESPA

THE COMPLETE HISTORY

Giorgio Sarti

75 YEARS
VESPA
THE COMPLETE HISTORY

GIORGIO NADA EDITORE

Giorgio Nada Editore

Editorial Coordination
Leonardo Acerbi

Editing
Giorgio Nada Editore

Graphic design
Isabella Gianazza
Sansai Zappini

Cover design
Sansai Zappini

Photo post-production
Nicola Dini

English translation
Neil Frazer Davenport

Photographs by
Antonio Corona
Cesare Resta
Giorgio Sarti
Paiggio Archive

Giorgio Nada Editore s.r.l.
Via Claudio Treves, 15/17
I - 20090 VIMODRONE - MI
Tel. +39 02 27301126
Fax +39 02 27301454
E-mail: info@giorgionadaeditore.it
www.giorgionadaeditore.it

The catalogue of Giorgio Nada Editore publications is available on request at the above address.

VESPA. 75 YEARS
ISBN: 9788879118552

To my wife Roberta.
She climbed onto my Vespa 200 Rally
for the first time in 1978.
And she is still riding with me.

Acknowledgements
I would like to thank the publisher, Giorgio Nada, for keeping faith over the years that have seen the birth of diverse editions of this book.
Warm thanks go to Luciano Greggio for his editorial coordination of the first edition in 2006, while I am similarly grateful to Leonardo Acerbi who has put up with me over the following editions.
Thanks also to Paolo Pezzini from the Piaggio Group
I would also like to remember Ing. Carlo Doveri who passed away in 2005

Distribution
Giunti Editore Spa
via Bolognese 165
I - 50139 FIRENZE
www.giunti.it

CONTENTS

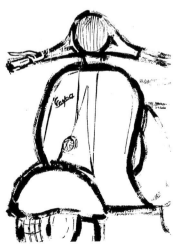

Piaggio celebrated the 60th anniversary of the birth of the Vespa on 27 April 2006. The ceremony was held at Pontedera in the Piaggio Museum, a place devoted to the conservation and promotion of the historical values of a vehicle that has represented – and above all continues to represent – extraordinary success in terms of design, research and technical innovation and creativity, labour and enterprise.

When Enrico Piaggio presented the first Vespa 98 to the public in 1946 and put the first 50 examples on sale, contemporary reports show that he received a very discouraging response from the experts. And yet, without hesitation, Piaggio the businessman decided to proceed with the production of a further 2,500 Vespas! It was a courageous move that paid spectacular dividends. Corradino D'Ascanio, the aeronautical engineer and inventor of the helicopter, was called upon to work swiftly and create a series of new models: the 98 was followed by the Vespa 125 introduced in 1949 and then by the Vespa U, the Vespa GS, the Vespone and numerous remarkable racing and trials prototypes. By 1952 the Pontedera-based company had already negotiated four foreign licences to satisfy growing demand for the vehicle, and by 1956 one million Vespas had been sold throughout the world. These were intense years in a country anxious to leave behind the drama of wartime destruction, a period in which a desire to construct and the challenge of the future were key elements in the success of not just Piaggio but other Italian businesses too.

The Vespa was born with the characteristic of originality and was proposed as a small, useful and attractive vehicle capable of responding to the economic and social changes that ranged from the period of construction through to the boom years of the Fifties and Sixties, from the uncertainties and difficulties of the Seventies to the triumph of the society of mass consumption. There are very few products that have managed to conserve their capacity for market penetration for so long: if it happens it is because those products express values capable of overcoming any barrier raised by changes in mentality, usage, taste or, more banally, obsolescence. Rather than merely enduring, the Vespa has proved capable of acting as a true protagonist of change, the interpreter of the dynamics of customs, aesthetics, language, fashion and the mentalities of men and women, adults and youngsters within the complex development of the economy and society.

While this is the story that has led to the construction of over 17 million Vespas, in one of the most recent economic and financial crises Piaggio risked going under and losing the patrimony of innovation and creativity embodied by the world's most popular scooter and shared by the other two-, three- and four-wheeled vehicles produced by the Piaggio Group.

That disaster was avoided. In fact, the changes in the structure of the company and the new management team have rapidly brought back into play those values rooted in the history and the abundance of ideas and skills represented by the men and women working at Pontedera; values they have successfully strengthened and renewed, giving a new impetus to the production process and, above all, to the thread of creativity, technological innovation, entrepreneurship and labour running through the creation of revolutionary new models that – today, just as 60 years ago – interpret when they do not anticipate the most modern demands for mobility and quality of life.

Giorgio Sarti's book, authoritatively published by Haynes in collaboration with Giorgio Nada Editore, and which it is my pleasure to commend, illustrates the various stages in the Vespa's history and documents the dynamics of a product that has become the stuff of legend and proved capable of retaining a leading position in its market sector. Above all, the book underlines the success of the Vespa, the evolution of an all-Italian project that has negotiated difficult times and today continues to represent the originality, the enterprise, the capacity for research and the achievements of Italian industry in the global economy.

For these reasons, the greatest tribute that we can pay to the first 60 glorious years of the Vespa – and to all its enthusiasts – is to plan for an equally extraordinary future.

Roberto Colaninno
President of the Piaggio Group

INTRODUCTION

In 1973 a very young Vespa enthusiast sent a proposal to the Piaggio management in Genoa for an advertising campaign based on the slogan: "Vespa, overtaking the times". The reply was a polite refusal: for this kind of thing there are advertising agencies, but thanks anyway. Satisfaction at having actually been contacted by the powers-that-be only partially made up for the disappointment at having been rejected. I know the story well, for I was that boy. My adolescent motorcycling development was, in fact, Vespa-based: a Vespa 50 Special at 14, a Vespa 125 Primavera at 16 and a Vespa 200 Rally at 18 years old. My relationship with the Vespa then cooled a little as more demanding motorcycles in terms of size, price and performance arrived, but I never lost my affection for Pontedera's jewel, quite the contrary. In 1984 came the pleasant surprise of a first prize in a Mondadori competition for the best film script based on the Vespa and a fine 125 PK Automatica found a place in my garage. I began to feel the appeal of the models of the past ever more strongly in the 1990s, pride of place now going to a perfectly preserved 1963 GL 150. As you might imagine, like any good enthusiast I have always collected all the books imaginable that featured the Vespa. However, I always felt something was missing; either they were too technical and written for restorers or they were too illustrative and lacked information. I never managed to find a single volume that would satisfy both the lover of a single model and an enthusiast capable of falling for a model in the legendary calendar. And so I set about the task myself and this is the result. It is just a shame the publisher politely rejected my suggested title: "Vespa, overtaking the times".

The author

A NOTE FOR READERS

This new book, *Vespa 75 Years. The complete history* is an update of the historical part of Giorgio Sarti's *Vespa 70. History, Technology, Models from 1946*, initially published back in 2006 and then updated and reprinted through to 2016. The extensive catalogue section that in the original work systematically recorded each individual model is now separately available as another book devoted to the Vespa legend, *Vespa. All the models*, published by Giorgio Nada Editore in 2020.

Part one

ORIGIN AND DEVELOPMENT

Birth and protagonists

Birth
and protagonists

12 o'clock midday, 23 April 1946, the patent office, Florence. Piaggio deposits the following patent: "Motorcycle with a rational arrangement of organs and elements, with a frame with mud-guards and covers concealing all mechanical parts."

Such was the official birth of the Vespa. Even though other scooters (vehicles with two small-diameter wheels) had already been built prior to the Second World War, there is no doubt that with the Vespa the genre took a significant step forward. Of significance in this respect is the wording of the official Piaggio press release. Firstly, the vehicle is deliberately described as a "motorcycle" because the scooters that had gone before had failed to leave a particularly positive impression. Above all, however, Piaggio was at pains to emphasise how the mechanical elements were fully enclosed by the side panels with the clear intent of drawing parallels between the new scooter and cars rather than traditional motorcycles.

It was no coincidence that the first prototype was presented on the Lancia stand at a motor show in November 1945. Enrico Piaggio was keen to associate the Vespa with a prestigious marque boasting a widespread and consolidated sales and distribution network. However, that attempt at an alliance with Lancia came to nothing, as was the

Piaggio & C.

The original "Società Rinaldo Piaggio" was founded by Rinaldo Piaggio at just 20 years of age in 1884. The next step was the limited partnership "Piaggio & C." established in 1897. The general partner was again Rinaldo Piaggio, with four partners: Oreste Odero (shipowner), Pietro Costa (sculptor) and Giacomo Pastorino (landowner). In the years 1892 and 1893 Rinaldo Piaggio bought out his partners and in 1920 relaunched the firm as "Piaggio & Compagno", with the "compagno" being Attilio Odero. Odero was a leading player: he was formerly the director of the Odero factory of Sestri Ponente before becoming the chairman of the Terni steelworks and founder of San Giorgio. He was to be the chairman of Piaggio & C. and remained in the position through to 1943. The company capital was increased from 15 million lire to 30 million in 1930. The following years of crisis reflected the American financial collapse of 1929: the company capital dropped in 1932 from 30 to 10 million lire, but Rinaldo Piaggio wisely decided to invest in human resources and brought a number of the most talented aeronautical engineers of the era to the company. They included: Giovanni Gabrielli, Giovanni Casiraghi and Corradino D'Ascanio, the man who was to play such a major role in the birth of the Vespa.

In 1934, the shareholders Rinaldo Piaggio and Attilio Odero were joined by Elena, the wife of Rinaldo. In 1936, a further six shareholders were added, the sons and son-in-laws of Rinaldo. On his death in 1938, the company capital was raised from 22.5 to 52.5 million lire. It was at this point that the two male heirs divided responsibilities for the company: the factories at Pisa and Pontedera in Tuscany being run by Enrico and those at Sestri and Finale Ligure in Liguria by Armando.

Birth and protagonists

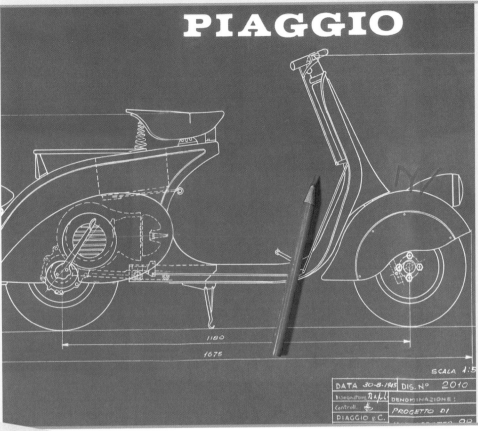

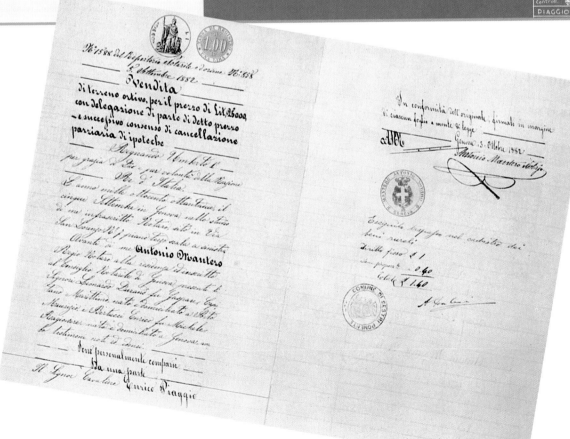

Enrico Piaggio signed off the birth of the Vespa in green crayon (30 August 1945).

The first and last page of the document relating to the purchase of the land on which the Piaggio factory at Sestri Ponente was built (3 October 1882).

Birth and protagonists

case with similar overtures made to Moto Guzzi, and Piaggio eventually decided to go it alone and organize the launch of the Vespa itself. The official presentation of the production model, the 98, took place at the prestigious Golf Club di Roma in the March of 1946, while in April the general public was able to admire the first Vespa at the Milan Trade Fair: a legend was born.

Piaggio then founded a company devoted exclusively to the distribution of the new scooter, "S.A.R.P.I." or Società Agenzie Rappresentanze Prodotti Industriali, and official sales of the Vespa were to begin.

Piaggio, more than just Vespa

Many enthusiasts are so accustomed to associating the manufacturer's name with that of the Vespa scooter that they assume the two came into being at the same time. In actual fact, by the time the Vespa was introduced Piaggio had already been in business for exactly sixty years.

The company took its name from Rinaldo Piaggio who was born in Genoa on the 15th of July 1864. At just twenty years of age he started his own woodworking business at Sestri Ponente. As increasingly significant orders began to be taken thanks to the skill

Two views of the Sestri Ponente factory during the woodworking period.

Birth and protagonists

of the company's craftsmen, Rinaldo Piaggio began to specialise in naval furnishings, obtaining numerous foreign commissions. In 1901, the workshop was enlarged and along with the joinery, metalworking began to be undertaken and the firm started building railway carriages. A natural follow-on from this was the production of trams and cable cars. During the First World War, Piaggio built anti-submarine motorboats but also began to devote resources to the field of aviation, firstly repairing engines and subsequently constructing aircraft. At the end of the war the company built an extremely advanced fighter, the P2, while in 1928 it inaugurated a facility for research into aerodynamics (in a wind tunnel) and hydrodynamics (using tanks). This period saw the birth of the P7, a sophisticated hydrofoil-equipped seaplane with two propellers for propulsion in both water and air.

During the 1930s, Piaggio engines conquered no less than 21 aviation world records, while the company continued to develop its railway carriages. The firm's founder, Rinaldo Piaggio, died in 1938 and was succeeded by his son Enrico. The Pontedera factory was bombed during the Second World War yet it was from the ruins that the scooter to be known as the Vespa emerged.

Among the Piaggio marine furnishings, of particular note was the salon created for the steamship Sicilia belonging to the Compagnia Navigazione Generale Italiana.

Birth and protagonists

Piaggio
at sea

Dozens of ships and motorboats boasted furnishings and fittings by Piaggio, 63 different vessels to be precise. Among the most important were the elegant passenger vessels, Cristoforo Colombo, Marco Polo, Galileo Galilei (Navigazione Generale Italiana) and Venezuela (Società la Veloce), the fast cruiser Liguria, the powerful battleships Giulio Cesare and Andrea Doria, the transatlantic liner Lorelei and a military vessel for the Imperial German Navy of Emperor Frederick.

Such was the quality of the firm's work that Piaggio was awarded prizes on the occasion of various international expositions: at Genoa in 1892, at Paris in 1900, at Milan 1906 and at Turin in 1911. With respect to the sawmill founded by his father Enrico, Rinaldo Piaggio's company expanded enormously and developed into one of the finest woodworking firms of the period.

One of the anti-submarine motorboats delivered to the Italian Navy during the *First World War and used in numerous missions in the Adriatic.*

Birth and protagonists

Piaggio
on rails

Early in the twentieth century the Italian railway was experiencing rapid growth, with the network in continual expansion. Piaggio constructed all kinds of railway rolling stock, from sophisticated first class luxury coaches to the spartan third class carriages, from post trains to goods wagons. In 1924, the company created a train for the king, the queen, the queen mother and the young prince, a commission worth no less than 6 million lire.

From 1937, Piaggio began constructing a seriess of sophisticated electric railcars and carriages in stainless steel under license from Budd of Philadelphia. The relative patents concerned above all the welding of the sheet metal and allowed a new generation of innovative and lightweight trains to be introduced.

The use of stainless steel guaranteed extended durability with no need for periodical maintenance or painting. An electric railcar, the MC2 (used by the Ferrovie Calabro-Lucane), is today exhibited at the entrance to the Piaggio Museum in Pontedera.

A tram built in great numbers by Piaggio for the city of Milan (left) and a postal wagon *with two axles that entered service in the early years of the 20th century.*

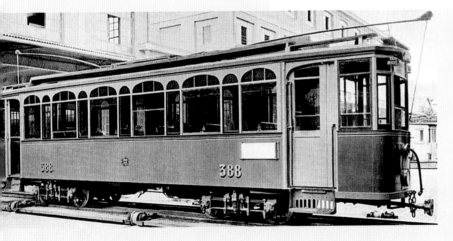
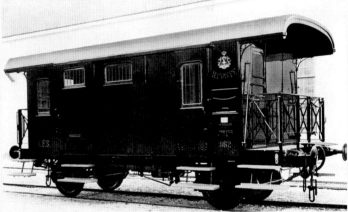

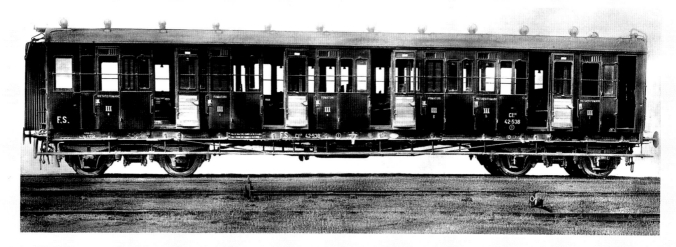

Birth and protagonists

Piaggio
and the
automobile

After having ranged throughout the transport sectors, it was only natural that Piaggio also began to think about motorcars too (Fiat was formed in 1899). Piaggio made contact with Mario Tolomei, then the De Dion Bouton and Motori Jupiter representative in Florence through his Società Italiana Costruzioni Automobili company. The agreement involved the construction of chassis at Pontedera together with the production of Jupiter engines under license. In the end, however, the negotiations broke down and nothing more was heard about Piaggio cars until the launch of the Vespa 400 in 1957.

Piaggio
in flight

While early in the twentieth century trains were still part of an innovative sector, aeroplanes represented a new frontier. Piaggio's aeronautical activities got underway in 1920 when Piaggio bought out Francesco Oneto's Pisa-based Officine Aeronautiche. The new company was constituted with capital of 10 million lire.

In 1923, Piaggio attempted to lure the great designer Giovanni Pegna away from the Pegna-Bonmartini aeronautical company. Faced with the straight refusal by Bonmartini who had no intention of losing an engineer of such prestige, Rinaldo Piaggio made him an offer he could hardly refuse: he would buy out Pegna-Bonmartini for the exorbitant

On the facing page, three examples of Piaggio railway rolling stock: a celebrated "Cento Porte" or "Hundred Doors" (top), the special carriage of the President of the Senate (centre) and the MC2 railcar of the Ferrovie Calabro-Lucane with a stainless steel body. Below, the first aircraft built under license by Piaggio in 1915, a Franco British Aviation seaplane.

Birth and protagonists

sum of 1,700,000 lire. The company further strengthened its position with the acquisition of Costruzioni Mecchaniche Nazionali and began producing radial engines. The most famous was the double row P XII RC with a total of no less than 18 cylinders and a maximum power output of 1750 hp, the most powerful piston engine ever built in Italy. 1938 saw the introduction of a particularly advanced four-engined aircraft, the P 108. Among the innovations that made it so sophisticated was a remote control system for the machine guns.

The P 148, designed by D'Ascanio and Casiraghi, was a training and aerobatic aircraft introduced in 1951. The first 70 examples were supplied to the Italian Air Force. A 5-seater version known as the P 149 was introduced in 1953. An example of the P 148 is on show in the Piaggio Museum forecourt in Pontedera.

It has been suggested on a number of occasions that when looking for a way of using a batch of aircraft engine starter motors that were lying redundant in the stores, Enrico Piaggio asked the engineer Corradino D'Ascanio to design a vehicle that could be powered by them. However, this is nothing more than unfounded legend.

It is true, however, that the auxiliary engines used for generators and compressors used to start Piaggio S.M. series aircraft shared the 98

The Piaggio P 3 biplane, powered by SPA 6A engines (top left). The Piaggio P 11 with a Lynk MK4 engine (top right). The Piaggio P 9 monoplane with a Circus MK2 engine (bottom left). In the mid-Thirties Piaggio abandoned wood and canvas construction in favour of all-metal frames (bottom right). On the facing page, a Dornier Wal built under license in 1926 (top); the Piaggio P 23 R from 1935 (centre) and the four-engined P 108 from 1938 (bottom).

Birth and protagonists

Birth and protagonists

engine's piston and connecting rod, but the crankcase of the motor/generator or motor/compressor assembly was a one-piece casting.

Piaggio
and
saucepans

In 1943, allied bombing flattened the Pontedera and Pisa factories. Only part of the 2100 machine tools used for building aircraft were saved in time, but it was thanks to that machinery that in 1945 the company was ready to initiate a new production venture. A new factory was raised on the ruins of the old one and the ex-combatants returning from the war turned up at the gates ready to work. But what were they to produce? It was up to Enrico Piaggio to shoulder this enormous responsibility. Given the post-war economic situation, the firm had to focus on a cheap consumer good for which there was, above all, widespread demand. The first idea that came to mind was… saucepans! Had Piaggio gone ahead and launched a range of kitchenware the Vespa would never have come into being. Fortunately, Enrico Piaggio had a corporate image to protect and could hardly afford to compromise the factory's prestigious reputation for producing trains and planes by making pots and pans. Perhaps if they had thought of some kind of vehicle instead…

The birth
of the Vespa

Italy in the period immediately following the Second World War was a shattered country. While there was a passionate desire for reconstruction, the problems to be overcome were immense and the workers were beginning to feel the effects of unemployment and inflation. Within this context Piaggio was facing severe difficulties. The bombing had destroyed much of the production facilities in both Liguria and Tuscany. At Pontedera (7000 employees and a covered area of 70,000 m^2) the greatest damage had been incurred by the foundries, the stores and the shipping department. The mechanical workshops were all but razed to the ground. In contrast, damage to the company's offices and administrative buildings was much less severe. Since 1943, the number of skilled workers employed by the Piaggio group had been reduced from 12000 to 2000, while the number of office staff had fallen from 2000 to 300. Thirty office staff and 60 workers remained at Pontedera.
The key to survival was the conversion from wartime to civil production, a problem faced by all those companies that had been engaged in the production of munitions. In a country strewn with rubble and that had yet to see the revival of an efficient public transport system, economic private transport was of primary importance. The bicycle was no longer sufficient over long distances, the motorcar was an absolutely inaccessible dream and the motorcycle was too adventurous for many. What was needed was… the Vespa!

Birth and protagonists

The desolate scene of the Piaggio factory following the heavy bombing of January 1944 (above). The Pontedera factory (below) seen from the sky in the 1950s.

Birth and protagonists

Corradino D'Ascanio

Corradino D'Ascanio was born at Popoli in the Abruzzo region on the 1st of February 1891. A flying enthusiast from a very early age, he attached a sail to a bicycle in an attempt to achieve lift-off. During the First World War, D'Ascanio made a name for himself with experiments with two-way radio equipment installed in aircraft. In 1918, he was appointed as head of the experimental department at Pomilio Brothers, an Italo-American aircraft factory located in Indianapolis. He designed and constructed modern fighters and bombers, but after the war Pomilio Brothers was unable to convert its military aircraft for civil use and the factory closed. D'Ascanio returned to his homeland and after having worked on a number of projects, focussed on his true passion, flight. In 1926, he designed and built his first helicopter, the DAT2, while in the early Thirties, thanks to financial backing from Baron Trojani, a prototype was constructed that immediately proved its potential by setting three world records. In spite of this promising debut, the D'Ascanio-Trojani company closed as a result of the problems caused by internal jealousies within the Italian air ministry. Moreover, an agreement signed by the Fiat president, Senator Giovanni Agnelli, also fell through as a result of Trojani's economic demands that were judged to be excessive. At least partial recompense for these disappoints came in 1933, when D'Ascanio was given a position at Piaggio. Here, his irreplaceable experience finally found the appropriate setting that would permit him to complete a number of aviation projects, above all in the field of helicopters. It was there that, at the end of the Second World War, Corradino D'Ascanio was asked to create a scooter that would permit mass mobility with an economical vehicle. Strange as it might seem, the enormous success of his Vespa was not a source of pride for Corradino D'Ascanio, but

The experiments conducted by Piaggio with pioneer helicopters dated from the second half of the 1920s with the DAT2 (D'Ascanio-Trojani) prototype equipped with fixed blades. The DAT3 (photo on this page) successfully flew between the 8th and 13th of October, establishing the world straight-line flight endurance record (8 minutes 34") at a height of 8 metres from the ground. Ing. D'Ascanio is portrayed in the photo at the bottom (second right) while the pilot seen aboard the helicopter is Major Marinello Nelli.

Birth and protagonists

ELICOTTERO "PD3.

rather one of irritation: for a designer who yearned for the sophisticated engineering of aviation projects, and above all helicopter design, having to take on a "simple", utilitarian two-wheeler must have represented a significant come-down.
Corradino D'Ascanio died at Pisa in 1981.

Corradino D'Ascanio's fame is naturally associated with his helicopters and the Vespa, but the dynamic inventor also explored a vast range of areas including:

- Perforated card calculators: (an "electro-pneumatic machine for the cataloguing and rapid research of documents" from 1925)
- Bread makers (an "electric oven for the baking of bread and pastries" from 1919)
- Fireworks ("delayed ignition fireworks for aircraft" from 1926)
- Cigarette holders with a timer (for personal use...)

D'Ascanio's memoirs recall his meeting with Enrico Piaggio:
On the way up to Biella I asked myself what it was he could want from me. I knew he had been reduced to making saucepans and I had no illusions: there would have been no talk of aeroplanes or helicopters. He welcomed me enthusiastically and said to me, «I want a vehicle that will put Italy on two wheels, but I don't want the usual motorcycle.» He then led me to a scooter built by a technician from Biella. Baptised as the Paperino [the Italian equivalent of Donald Duck], it was derived from an unsuccessful light motorcycle born in 1940 in Turin. Then again, there had been numerous scooters: Krupp built one in 1919, the French and the English in 1920. But they had not been successful. And were too expensive. They had not been designed for mass production. This Paperino too closely resembled a motorcycle and Piaggio rejected it. I knew nothing about motorcycles. That is to say, I knew

motorcycles from the outside, but I had never had anything to do with their engineering. Moreover, as vehicles they did not appeal to me at all and I had never ridden one. I tried to play for time, but Piaggio would not give me any. He had intuited that in order to escape from post-war stagnation, the average Italian would have to overcome, among many others, one enormous obstacle: that of traffic. Individual traffic. Piaggio wanted to solve the problem and realised that the future of his company depended on it.

On the facing page, two sketches drawn in the Piaggio offices of the PD3 helicopter prototype for which D'Ascanio devised an extremely elongated fuselage, at the end of which was located a second small propeller, while the principal, large diameter horizontal rotor was set towards the front (photo on this page). Bottom right, the PD4 prototype from 1952 with two twin-bladed contra-rotating rotors.

Corradino D'Ascanio

(From the Piaggio Magazine, year 1, number 1, January 1949):
Not knowing motorcycles, I was in the ideal position to create a vehicle without precedents. Piaggio was counting on this. «Only you can tackle the problem with a wholly new outlook» he told me. I followed intuitive criteria. I felt that the machine ought to serve those who, like me, had never ridden a motorcycle and hated the machine's lack of manoeuvrability. I thought it over for a while and one Sunday the basic idea came to me. The most important factor was being able to mount the vehicle comfortably, something that had already been resolved with the ladies' bicycle. So I started out with the concept that is fundamental in the ladies' bicycle. I felt that a seated position was more comfortable and more rational than having to straddle the frame. Then we had to make it as manoeuvrable as possible. We had to take into consideration its urban use. It had to be ridden without taking one's hands from the handlebars. How could this be done? Simple, I put the gearshift on the handlebar. Another thing: it should not dirty hands and trousers, one of the most conspicuous inconveniences with motorcycles. My motorcycle therefore had to have a covered engine isolated from the rider: a single assembly with the rear wheel. As a consequence, I created a transmission with no chain, the in-line gearbox being incorporated in the engine-wheel assembly. Another feature was dictated by my aeronautical experience: the mono-strut support for the front wheel rather than the bicycle-derived fork. Moreover, I introduced an innovatory monocoque body, eliminating the tubular system. In aeronautics there is a dogma among designers: lightness does not prejudice strength, as long as you do not go too far. Another requirement: the spare wheel. Remembering that on many occasions, travelling by car, I had seen motorcyclists at the side of the road struggling with a punctured inner tube removed from the wheel, I decided that all in all a mere puncture should not be a problem requiring a mechanic. I wanted my motorcyclist to have something in common with car drivers. In short, I was trying to build the machine as simply as possible. One of my favourite maxims has always been that of old Henry Ford: «if you don't fit it, it won't break».

The prototype Vespa came together in a flash. The engineering difficulties, and there were more than a few, in part because a brand-new approach was required, were overcome with a rapidity unthinkable today. The fact is that some of my assistants had worked with me for years and I had workers who had understood the importance of the vehicle and were determined to make ita success. There was a great desire to lift ourselves above the ruins of the war, to rise again, to serve a cause that was actuallya common cause, not just that of the owner. We all knew our future was at stake. My innovations were noted and admired. The more innovations I presented, the more the enthusiasm of the workforce grew.

A miracle took place in Biella. The proof is here: between the design and the construction of the first examples to be tested passed just three months. The Vespa, which initially had an engine of Sachs derivation, was tested in the September of 1945.

Facing page, D'Ascanio proudly poses alongside a first generation Vespa and (on this page), the father of the Vespa portrayed on the occasion of the production of the millionth example (April 28 1946).

Birth and protagonists

Carlo Carbonero

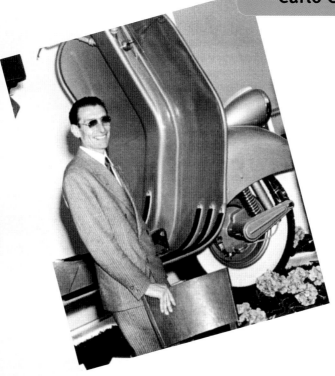

The engineer Carlo Carbonero, a talented aero-engine designer who worked closely with Corradino D'Ascanio, made a highly significant contribution to the development of the Vespa. The "father" of the Vespa frequently recalled how useful Carbonero's assistance was in the creation of the prototype. «Once the design had been defined, the prototype was constructed in record-breaking time thanks to the dynamism and the intelligent collaboration of Carlo Carbonero. I remember that one morning I presented the engineer with a drawing of a wheel and by that same evening the wheel was already made! And it was the engineer Carbonero himself who personally tested the prototype on the 4th of November 1945.»

Francesco Lanzara

The engineer Francesco Lanzara, born in Naples in 1914, played a significant role in the Piaggio story. He graduated in civil engineering in Naples in 1936 and in aeronautical engineering in Rome in 1940. He met Rinaldo Piaggio in Africa and subsequently became director of the Pontedera factory for over 30 years from 1946 to 1979. When he joined the company he was given the unenviable task of organizing all production in the factory. The magnitude of this undertaking in the post-war years and the passage from industrial reconversion to subsequent expansion can only be imagined. However, Lanzara's affinity with the Piaggio board meant that he was able to express his great talent to best effect and it was at least in part thanks to his managerial contribution that Piaggio was able to operate rapidly and efficiently.

Birth and protagonists

In search
of a market

Now that the Vespa was born, Piaggio was faced with the by no means easy problem of how to distribute it. The first idea was that of associating it with established marques with which it could share the same "shop window". And which was the name of the moment in those years? The celebrated Moto Guzzi, of course, a company that could also boast an established distribution network.

In any case, the question was resolved almost before it had been posed: at Mandello, Count Parodi refused any form of commercial agreement. He had no faith in the so-called small-wheeled vehicles and the new scooter was seen as an inevitable commercial fiasco.

Despite this setback, Piaggio continued in his attempts to find a partner by aiming even higher through an association with the world of luxury cars. Contacts were made with the Lancia sales network and following a positive response the wonders of the new scooters were explained to the dealers one by one. Many were attracted by the idea, but again the initiative soon collapsed: sales were poor, well below expectations. At this point Piaggio decided to go it alone and thanks in part to successful advertising campaigns and the possibility of hire purchase the situation was overturned.

The first advertisements with which the Vespa 98 was launched also carried *the names of the first distributors of Piaggio's new product.*

Birth and protagonists

35 YEARS IN THE PIAGGIO TECHNICAL DEPARTMENT

Carlo Doveri was born at Viareggio in 1923. He graduated in engineering from the University of Pisa, a student of Corradino D'Ascanio. When this last moved to Piaggio he asked Doveri if he would like to follow him. Doveri accepted the offer and joined the Pontedera firm in 1950. He remained in the technical department through to 1984 and then worked a further two years as a consultant. In short, a 35-year career at the forefront of Vespa technical development.

Q. Engineer Doveri, what were your first tasks at Piaggio?

A. *I joined Piaggio in 1950 and immediately worked on an aeronautical problem: the in-flight measurement of stress on metal aircraft propeller blades. I remember that we had to fabricate manifolds with special bladed channels with mercury, not an easy problem but one we resolved satisfactorily.*

Q. And with regard to the Vespa?

A. *I was working on the Vespa too at the same time. I worked on the flexible cable gear change in place of the so-called "rod" system. A propos of this, I remember that Engineer D'Ascanio was so keen to see this feature finished that he chewed me out because I kept him waiting for an hour. And yet I'd got to the office by 7.30 in the morning! It was just that he'd got there by 6.30... I also worked on the carburettors that tended to ice up in the winter. We created an aluminium manifold that would channel warm air over them.*

The author with engineer Doveri during the interview held at his Pontedera office.

Q. You had direct contacts with Enrico Piaggio as well as Corradino D'Ascanio. What were their characters like?

A. *They both had very determined characters. D'Ascanio was always calm, but when he did get riled it was rough. Enrico Piaggio certainly knew his business. When Enrico Piaggio asked D'Ascanio if he could work on the Paperino, he refused because it had been created by another engineer. So Piaggio spluttered, «you're as stubborn as ever! Do what you want, but do something!»*

Q. What was the standard of training of your immediate colleagues?

A. *Extremely high. You could see that their aeronautical experience had instilled in all of them the need to work to the highest qualitative levels. In aeronautics it is simply a question of pure safety, but transferring these skills to a vehicle as spartan as this meant that the Vespa was born well, with no defects. The "mentality" was right for doing things well.*

Q. Who chose the colour for the first Vespa?

A. *Enrico Piaggio himself. At that time he though like Ford: any colour as long as it was green.*

Q. Before joining Piaggio had you ever tried riding a scooter?

A. *Actually, yes... A scooter I built myself. I called it "Cleofe" and it was powered by a British Jap 100 engine. I later also installed a Vespa engine.*

Q. And had you already had a chance to try a Vespa?

A. *Yes, I remember I'd ridden one belonging to a friend when I lived at Aosta. I liked the engine, the roadholding a little less.*

Q. How was the experimental department organized?

A. In effect, there were two. One smaller one directed by Fausto Taranto where parts were worked on directly, without drawings. There were just a few workers here, but all highly skilled and used little machinery, a lathe, a milling machine. But they knew how to do everything. Then there was the experimental department proper directed by Averaldo Martini where projects were designed.

Q. One of the most important technical modifications was that of the passage from a 5% oil-fuel mixture to a 2% mix. Were there any problems?

A. We called it "DR" for distribuzione rotante or rotary valve. Initially we couldn't work out why the con-rod roller bearing was always wearing out. Especially given that the same defect never occurred with the 400 light car. What was happening was that the air-petrol flow was not heated and reached the crankcase directly. When cold the residual oil lacked viscosity and the rollers consequently wore. We then found out that the only difference was that in the case of the 400, the rollers were caged while the others were not. All it took was to use caged bearings and the problem was solved.

Q. Did you ever get to test any Vespas personally?

A. Yes, even though we generally relied on testers. In fact, I could tell some stories…

Q. Please do…

A. The ones who crashed too often we'd send to other departments, that of the Ape or the Hydrojet for example. At that time we would stage events to demonstrate the potential of jet thrust, with no propellers, even setting up jumps from a ramp. One time the tester, Natale Biasci, took the ramp at high speed but sideways and completed a full spin before touching down perfectly on the water. Everybody applauded enthusiastically thinking it had all been planned and he raised his arms in triumph. But when we saw in him in flight we had our hands in our hair!

Q. Other episodes…

A. One day the tester, Cau, had a terrible accident, crashing head-on with the Vespa into a car coming the other way. But he completed a somersault in mid-air and landed practically on his feet, unhurt. So then he goes up to the driver of the car, who in the meantime had stopped, white in the face, convinced he'd killed him. When Cau smiled at him, knocking on the window, the driver fainted from the shock. Well, when the ambulance arrived they picked up the guy who was driving the car, still unconscious…

Q. The Vespa sidecar: where were the sidecars built?

A. We didn't build them directly. They were made by an outside firm in Turin. In fact, here at Piaggio, we didn't even assemble them. We sent the Vespas to Turin and they saw to marketing them.

Q. You spent a lot of time on the Vespa 400, didn't you?

A. Yes. I worked at the Fourchambault factory for some time. I have to say they loved the Vespa even more than Pontedera did. They even built a monument to the Vespa.
The Vespa 400 really was a good design; above all, it weighed a good two quintals (200 kg) less than the Fiat 500. But it was never supported by adequate marketing. There was talk of a joint venture with Peugeot, but Enrico Piaggio didn't want to be tied down. It was also sold in the United States, Great Britain and Germany. But of course, with a single model you couldn't do much more. In recompense, the 400 that participated in the Monte Carlo Rally did 140 kph!

Q. At ACMA in France, they also built the famous military Vespa.

A. Yes, but it was a project developed by Giorgio D'Ascanio, son of the great Corradino.

Q. At one time the Vespa was presented at shows with veritable special effects…

A. Yes, and they were stunning. Once we had it moving on its own on a sheet of glass. But the true showstopper was when we had it moving, again on its own, on a wire! This was possible thanks to a gigantic gyroscope occupying the full width of the body. At the end of the wire the Vespa went behind a door, the gyroscope recharged and the Vespa came out again!

Q. Who came up with these ideas?

A. What a question, Corradino D'Ascanio of course!

Q. The best of the Vespa models constructed?

A. The PX, without doubt. A true distillation of all the experience gained previously. Apart from a minor aerodynamic problem, it was practically perfect straight out of the box.

Q. What problem was that?

A. There was a certain instability especially in the slipstream of other vehicles. We even went to the Fiat Research Centre in Turin to study the aerodynamics in the wind tunnel. We conducted an analysis with a gyroscopic platform and we realised that the problem stemmed from the handlebar set too far away. The rider was inadvertently moving the handlebar because his arms were over-extended. All we had to do was set the handlebar further back and the problem disappeared.

Q. Let's talk about the Moscone, the outboard motor: was it a success or a fiasco?

A. Neither one nor the other. What's certain, however, is that it was launched too early and then when we'd finished producing it there was a boom in recreational boating…□

Birth and protagonists

Enrico Piaggio

Enrico Piaggio was born in Pegli in 1905. He graduated in Economics and Commerce from the University of Genoa in 1927 and received an honorary degree in engineering from the University of Pisa in 1951. He died in Pisa in 1965. The following obituary was published in the Vespa Club d'Italia magazine No. 162 in 1965: Enrico Piaggio, the father of the Vespa, of the Vespa Club of Italy, is dead. Enrico Piaggio, generous supporter and constant benefactor, but also the figure spiritually closest to our endeavours and an understanding, enthusiastic participant in our associative passions despite being so averse to all forms of exhibitionism. Even from a distance, he always took an interest in the birth and development of our club and never failed to appreciate its efforts and to take pride in the successes that have marked the Vespa Club of Italy and of

Europe's 16 years. We remember him present at the start of the first 1000 km race at Brescia, wishing the Vespisti, one sportsman to another, good luck for the race, and we remember him happy and smiling at the Viareggio conference celebrating the tenth anniversary of the Vespa Club of Italy; the long applause of all the delegates touched him and showed him both how sincere that wave of affection actually was and how he was recognised as the artificer and moving spirit behind the many celebratory events that had been held in Italy and elsewhere in Europe thanks to "his" Vespa and in the name of concord and fraternity between peoples of different nationalities and languages. Once again, at a now long past Conference of the Vespa Club of Europe at San Remo, on the occasion of the first Eurovespa, Enrico Piaggio joined the Vespisti present and felt vibrate

Enrico Piaggio and his wife Donna Laura – early Fifties – on the occasion of an event celebrating the extraordinary success of the

Vespa. Behind them, with glasses, Renato Tassinari, the volcanic founder and chairman of the Vespa Club.

in his great heart the affectionate enthusiasm and the fervid support of the representatives of all the Vespisti of Europe. He gracefully accepted the title of honorary member of the Vespa Club of Europe and belonged to the select group of founders of the Vespa Club of Italy. He had always believed in the rise of the Vespa Club and in its beneficial social role, above and beyond any propagandistic goal and he wanted the Vespa Club to unite young people and enthusiasts of the small engine in a harmonious and attractive touristic and sporting activity. The Vespisti of all the nations of Europe knew him, we felt him present and alive at our races and rallies and would always acknowledge him with an affectionate salute. Excited, we would always remember him when witnessing the endless parades of Vespisti in a festival of sun and flags, along the broad avenues of Madrid, or the boulevards of Paris through to the vastness of the Champs Elyseés, along the streets of Rome on the occasion of the Olympic Games. Along the avenues of Salzburg and Munich, along the roads winding through the Dolomites to Misurina and Cortina, along the roads of England and Switzerland, "Dottor Piaggio" would never be far from our thoughts, we always hoped that he would be present and that he would share with us the joy of those festive and triumphant sights that were, after all, the remarkable result of all his determined, intelligent work. We would lay on his table, on our return, photographs of numerous events, myriad landscapes and picturesque scene in which the Vespista appeared as a victorious protagonist. He would hide his deep satisfaction with a quick, «good, good», and as if looking at those photos was a frivolous distraction he would add «and now let's get down to work» and tackle the more pressing problems of the great industrialist. Enrico Piaggio lives on among all Vespisti with his unforgettable smile of intelligent integrity.

A number of shots of Enrico Piaggio during the years in which he led the company to the conquest of the domestic market with the Vespa, the revolutionary scooter that changed the lives of millions of people throughout the world. He was also an enlightened businessman in the social field, constructing the modern Piaggio village.

Birth and protagonists

Umberto Agnelli

Umberto Agnelli was born at Lausanne in Switzerland on the 1st of November 1934. He was the last of Edoardo Agnelli and Virginia Bourbon del Monte's seven children. Umberto was just a year old when his father died and was eleven when he lost his mother. His brother Gianni was his elder by 13 years and it was he who was the first to take up the company reins. Umberto graduated in law and at 22 years of age took on his first important position when he became president of the Juventus football club.

On the 15th of June 1959, in the chapel on the Piaggio estate at Veramista (near Pontedera) Umberto married Antonella Bechi Piaggio. In 1962 he became chairman of SAI (the insurance company) and in 1964 was appointed head of Fiat France. In 1965 he became chairman of Piaggio & C., the first successor to Enrico Piaggio. A year later the Era River broke its banks, the ensuing floods causing great damage to the Pontedera works. The restoration phase was to be one of the key episodes in Umberto Agnelli's chairmanship at Piaggio. He himself recalled the workforce's great commitment to the restarting of production in the shortest possible time. In particular, the shutting down of the furnaces (which might have exploded) is always cited as one of the events that made the greatest impression on him. In the early years of his chairmanship, the structure of the Piaggio firm remained virtually unchanged, both in terms of organization and production. Given their consummate technical skills, both Corradino D'Ascanio (Technical Department) and Francesco Lanzara (factory director) were naturally retained. In the late Sixties, Umberto Agnelli nonetheless began to appoint new members to the board of directors in order to form a broader group with greater attention to diversified activities. In 1970

he was appointed as managing director of Fiat. In 1974 he separated from Antonella Piaggio and married Allegra Caracciolo. In 1980 Umberto was appointed vice president of Fiat. In the 1990s he had operational responsibility for IFI and IFIL (the family treasure chests). He was appointed president of Fiat in 2003, an hour after the death of his brother Gianni (on the 24th of January). However, a little over a year later, on the night of the 27th of May 2004, Umberto passed away at his Mandria estate near Turin. He was 69 years old.

ANTONELLA BECHI PIAGGIO
Antonella was the daughter of Colonel Alberto Bechi. During the war, Bechi was dismissed by Galeazzo Ciano for having covered his photo during a meeting and a few days after the armistice he was killed in a fire fight in Sardinia. His widow remarried Enrico Piaggio who "adopted" the little Antonella. At 20 years of age, Antonella married Umberto Agnelli. In an interview by Oriana Fallaci published by L'Europeo, Antonella Bechi Piaggio declared: «They've said that it's a six-wheeled marriage, or that it's not a marriage but an industrial agreement. I don't even bother getting angry. It's such a stupid argument. I've loved Umberto since I was ten years old. I'd always thought we would get married and our families knew nothing: so why would they say it was them who organized everything?».

However, the marriage only lasted 14 years and in 1973 Umberto and Antonella separated in great secrecy. It was again in secret that in 1974 Umberto married Allegra Caracciolo di Castagneto (cousin of Marella Caracciolo, wife of Gianni Agnelli) at Villar Perosa, while Antonella married Umberto Visconti di Modrone.

Giovanni Alberto Agnelli

Giovanni Alberto Agnelli was president of Piaggio from 1988 through to his premature death in 1997 at just 36 years of age. From the outset he emphasised the "three missions": internationalization, innovation and ethics.

The first objective, that of expanding the markets, was explained with an anecdote: «I'd like to quote a personal example. I have a watch that I wear frequently and that once belonged to my grandfather, Enrico Piaggio. It was presented to him in 1955, on the occasion of the 100,000th Vespa sale on the South African market. 38 years have passed and we no longer sell anything in South Africa».

The second objective was that of making Piaggio a leading company in the search to find innovative solutions to the problems of personal urban transport, without losing contact with the environment.

The third objective was making sure that Piaggio was distinguished not only as an innovative company, but also as an ethical, transparent and collaborative company capable of generating a profound sense of shared objectives at all levels: «In sign of a continuity with the traditions, values and culture that have enabled it to grow. In the interests of the company, of those who work for it and of the shareholders. But also, and above all, in the interest of our country.»

Giovanni Alberto Agnelli was keen to reinforce Piaggio's roots and to create a strong sense of belonging. «Attachment to the company is long–held value at Piaggio».

Nominated as president of the group in 1988, Giovanni Alberto Agnelli succeeded his father Umberto who handed over the reins to the company after 23 years. His presence contributed to a revolution within the company, with an emphasis on the strategic importance of the concept of globalization: «This is no trend of the moment. In order to be a leading company we have to expand in the area accounting for over 80% of the market. Europe, our domestic market on which we are incontrovertibly the

protagonists, represents just 12% of the global market. Restricting ourselves to Europe signifies being excluded from this market, a situation that within a few years would signify the absolute loss of competitiveness».

The Vespa beyond 2000

In the December of 1999, a remarkable piece of news spread among Vespa enthusiasts and the financial world: Piaggio was being "sold". The purchasers were the Morgan Grenfell Investment Funds, a subsidiary of Deutsche Bank, with 81.5% and the Texas Pacific Group (TPG) with 8.5% of the capital. The remaining 10% remained in the hands of Umberto Agnelli.

This was an important event in the history of the company, that through a strong shareholding could set ambitious objectives such as, for example, a return to the American market (abandoned in the 1980s) or flotation on the stock exchange. That the management structure remained Italian and production continued at Pontedera was evidence of the new investors' appreciation of the way the firm's business had been conducted through to the acquisition. The third millennium was to see Piaggio launch numerous new models and continue the development of new power units with increasingly innovative features oriented towards extremely low pollution levels. Another significant event was the revival of the Gilera marque, not only with scooters but also large motorcycles such as the 600 presented at the Milan Motorcycle Show in the September of 2001.

Joint statement by Piaggio and Deutsche Morgan Grenfell, the 16th of December 1999:

"The operation leading to the acquisition of a controlling share in Piaggio & C. S.p.A., the European leader on the two-wheeled vehicle market, was concluded today. Morgan Grenfell Private Equity (MGPE) shall control 81.5% of Piaggio, Dr. Umberto Agnelli shall retain 10%, while 8.5% of the capital shall be held by the Texas Pacific Group (TPG). MPGE shall involve a number of selected international financial investors and Mediocredito Lombardo. With managed capital of over 1.8 billion dollars, MGPE is one of the largest private equity funds in Europe. Since its constitution, MGPE has completed 478 investments for an overall value of 9 billion dollars. Mediocredito Lombardo (the merchant bank of the Gruppo Intesa), which will hold a 4.5% share of Piaggio, is responsible for the structuring of the entire operation and has organized credit lines made available by Banca Intesa to support Piaggio's development plans in view of its great opportunities for growth. Today, the assembly of Piaggio and CSPA shareholders nominated the new board of directors which confirmed Ing. Alessandro Barberis as chairman of the company and Ing. Rosselli del Turco as managing director and general director; on the same occasion Dott. Razzano was nominated vice - president.

Birth and protagonists

The Colaninno
Era

In the September of 2003, Vespa returned to Italian hands. An important financial operation was concluded that saw control of Piaggio pass from Deutsche Morgan Grenfell to IMMSI, a real estate company owned by the Mantuan financier Roberto Colaninno. The agreement involved the constitution of a new Dutch de jure company (local law permits shares to be differentiated on the basis of a right to vote), Piaggio Holding B.V. The company capital is constituted by four classes of shares (A, B, C, and D) with different company and administrative rights. IMMSI invested 100 million euros in the operation and holds 100% of the Class A shares. This constitutes 31.25% of the company capital and provides a majority vote and a majority of board members.

The new chairman of Piaggio is Roberto Colaninno himself, while the managing director is Rocco Sabelli. The group's debt was reduced thanks to the 100 million euro cash injection by Colaninno and the 150 million converted into shares by the creditor banks. The agreement between Piaggio and IMMSI was not easy to reach. The previous year an agreement had been signed whereby Piaggio was to have acquired the MV Agusta marque, but the operation was never concluded.

Roberto Colaninno (on the left in the photo), the new chairman of Piaggio, celebrates *the acquisition of the company with Rocco Sabelli, the new managing director.*

Birth and protagonists

The acquisition of Piaggio by IMMSI: the official communication (*Piaggiornale*, No. 10, October 2003)

Milan, 23 October 2003

Following the execution of the company procedures requested, today saw the closing of the contract signed on the 24ᵗʰ of September 2003 between IMMSI SpA, the "Dep IV" fund (managed by Morgan Grenfell Private Equity Ltd), Morgan Grenfell Development Capital Syndications Ltd (a company forming part of the Deutsche Bank Group), Piaggio Holding SpA and PB srl, a company constituted by the Piaggio Group's financing banks. Transfer of control over the management of Piaggio group affairs in Italy and abroad thus becomes operational.

The shareholders' assembly of Piaggio & C. SpA, the company dealing with all the group's industrial and operational affairs, has nominated the new board of directors, on which IMMSI has a majority of seats. This board will remain in force for three years, through to the approval of the balance sheet on the 31ˢᵗ of December 2005, and is composed as follows: Roberto Colaninno (nominated as chairman by the assembly), Rocco Sabelli, Luciano La Noce, Giorgio Magnoni, Matteo Colaninno, Pietro Faraoni, Gaetano Miccichè, Graham Clemson and Vincenzo de Bustis Figarola. The board subsequently nominated Rocco Sabelli as managing director.

Within the new structure of the group, Piaggio is wholly controlled by the newly-formed Dutch de jure company Piaggio Holding Netherlands B.V., which has entirely subscribed an increase in Piaggio & C. SpA capital for a total of 235 million euros following debt restructuring with the creditor banks. With a patrimony of 320 million euros, Piaggio Holding Netherlands B.V. is itself controlled by IMMSI SpA (31.25%), a company constituted by the former Piaggio Holding SpA and by other shareholders. IMMSI has a majority of voting rights in the Piaggio Holding Netherlands B.V. assembly, as well as a majority among the members of the firm's Supervisory Board composed of Roberto Colaninno (President), Rocco Sabelli, Luciano La Noce, Michele Colaninno, Carlo d'Urso, Teresio Testa, Patrizio Menchetti, Graham Clemson and Diarmuid Cummins.

Birth and protagonists

IMMSI
consolidates
control

IMMSI becomes majority shareholder Official communication (*Piaggiornale*, No. 11/12 November/December 2004)

Milan 28 December

IMMSI SpA, the holding company controlling the Piaggio Group, announces that it has acquired for 45 million euros, within the ambit of the Aprilia operation, 28,334 class C shares in Piaggio Netherlands B.V. held by Scooter Holding 3 B.V., the company bringing together the former Piaggio shareholders. Following the operation, which will also involve a 50 million euro capital injection in Piaggio & C. SpA., Piaggio Netherlands B.V. will own 86.9% of Piaggio & C. SpA. Following this acquisition, IMMSI, which already holds a majority of the voting rights in Piaggio Netherlands B.V. and in Piaggio and C. SpA, saw its capital holding in Piaggio Netherlands B.V. grow from 31.25% to 40%, thus becoming the majority shareholder in the holding company controlling the Piaggio Group.

The growth of IMMSI's share of Piaggio capital is in line with the Pontedera group's industrial development plans both in Italy and abroad, and permits a significant valorisation of the potential of the IMMSI investment, especially in view of the future quotation of the Piaggio Group on the stock exchange.

A colossus
with five
two-wheeler
marques

The Italian two-wheeler industrial pole was born in 2005: Piaggio acquired 100% of the Aprilia Group (which in turn comprised the Moto Guzzi and Laverda marques). The figures are significant: a turnover of 1.5 billion euros, a 24% share of the European market and 35% in Italy. The group has a production capacity of over 600,000 vehicles a year and employs over 6000 men and women. It has eight factories around the world, six research centres and is present in 50 countries. It is the world's fourth largest motor- cycle group. The terms of the operation provide for the subscription of the entire Aprilia capital increase of 50 million euros, subject to the making good of all losses (amounting to 108 million euros) at 31 October 2004 and the zeroing of the company capital. Piaggio takes over credit extended by the banks to Aprilia amounting to 98 million euros and issues in favour of the same banks to a maximum value of 64 million euros. The bank credit lines of the Aprilia Group were restructured for 78 million euros, of which 70 million with a duration extended to seven years and at market rates and the remainder with a short-term credit line.

Part two

ORIGIN AND DEVELOPMENT

Technical and styling evolution

Technical and styling evolution

Over its first 70 years the Vespa has obviously evolved, yet has always managed to remain true to itself. The less that was changed the better, in fact. At a certain point, Piaggio actually decided it could do without the Vespa name (introducing the Cosa in the 1990s), but was eventually obliged to make an about turn. The Vespa is the Vespa, it would be like changing the taste of Coca Cola. The Vespa scooter is a very special industrial product that half a century after its introduction has the extremely rare privilege of being "updated" with a series of features that deliberately introduced stylistic elements from the past. In order to celebrate the 2006 anniversary, for example, the headlight was mounted on the front mudguard, a reference to the 98 model from 1946.

The scooter's technical evolution can be divided into two fundamental periods. The first lasted no less than 50 years and focussed on the single-cylinder two-stroke engine. This configuration signified particularly simple engineering, but also high atmospheric pollution values. From the 50th anniversary in 1996, the engine adopted was a more sober and sophisticated four-stroke unit and it is right to speak of a second life for the Vespa. In that first period, the two-stroke engine was developed continuously, but the evolution was a slow

The basic concept of the new scooter was established in the very first sketches by Ing.

D'Ascanio and the vehicle went into production in the spring of 1946 under the Vespa name.

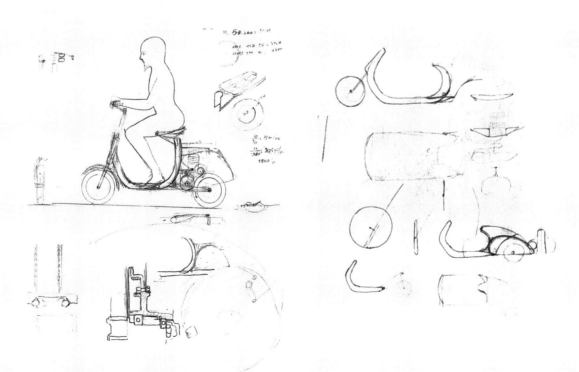

Technical and styling evolution

and gradual process. One particularly important innovation was the passage from a 5% to a 2% oil-fuel mixture, with a significant reduction in exhaust smoke, dirt and coking. Another key episode in the development of the two-stroke was the introduction of the automatic premixer. The fuel system continued to feature a carburettor through to the introduction of the 250 and the adoption of sophisticated fuel injection. A manual gearbox was retained into the third millennium, but automatic transmission began to be offered from the 1980s onwards. It was initially regarded with a certain diffidence, but by the 1990s few were prepared to do without it. With regard to the frame, there were no true generational revolutions. The bodywork composed of the steel monocoque is a common denominator for all models, an element of distinction with the competition offering tubular frames with plastic body panels. The side-panels were originally removable and later fixed, but this was a detail that hardly overturned the original design. Over the years, the wheels were increased in diameter from 8" to 10", at which point they remained for a long period. Only in the third millennium have we seen the introduction of 11" and 12" wheels. The suspension also evolved, although without straying far from the configuration adopted in the 1940s with a trailing link at the front.

The experimental models

A three-wheeled Vespa
Among the many projects developed at Piaggio, those concerning the three-wheeled Vespa were without doubt the most original. The project was born in 1950 when Giorgio D'Ascanio tested a version of the Vespa fitted with a kind of hood as protection from the rain. The testers noted a certain difficulty in holding the road in the case of turbulence such as when they were passed by a truck at a certain speed. In order to retain the advantages of protection without losing stability, in 1953 it was decided to construct a prototype Vespa with three wheels, two at the back, one at the front; of the two rear wheels, only one was driven.

However, as the vehicle was less stable than expected, a second prototype was constructed in 1955 with two wheels at the front using arms and rockers. This design proved to be effective but a little too complex and was therefore abandoned. The Paris-Dakar rally held largely in Africa became famous in the early '80s. It was and continues to be a gruelling test for competitors and their machinery. Piaggio built a prototype featuring a supplementary tank to extended the vehicle's range and allow great distances to be covered between refuelling stops. Tyres with an aggressive tread pattern were fitted to cope with the rough terrain. The prototype remained a one-off, however.

The '40s

Engine

The first engine fitted to the 98 had a modest power output of just 3.2 hp at 4,500 rpm. With the successive 125 the output rose to 4.5 hp at the same engine speed. The power unit was a horizontal, single-cylinder, two-stroke with three ports (intake, transfer and exhaust) and a deflector piston. Cooling was taken care of with a forced air system using a fan mounted on the flywheel magneto and a manifold on the cylinder head and barrel assembly. Cylinder head and piston were in light alloy, while the cylinder barrel was in cast-iron. The fuel system featured a Dell'Orto TA 17 carburettor and used a 5% oil-fuel mix. Ignition was via a flywheel magneto. The clutch was a multiplate oil bath unit. The gearbox had three speeds, with a handlebar grip-shift and rigid control rods. The transmission to the rear wheel was direct, with an intermediate flexible coupling.

The engine-transmission assembly was a simple, robust unit, exactly what was required in those years. Virtually everything was constructed in-house, with just two components being brought in from external suppliers: the carburettor (Dell'Orto) and the sparkplug (Marelli). The forced air cooling absorbed power and was an added complication, but proved to be necessary. The prototype, which relied on vents on the engine cover, was in fact subject to overheating.

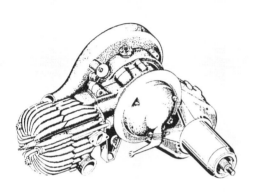

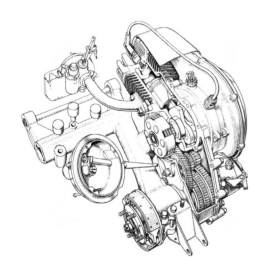

Technical and styling evolution

Frame, suspension, brakes and wheels

The steel frame constituted the Vespa's most characteristic element, so much so that its structure was to remain substantially unaltered throughout the scooter's production life. It was a true monocoque and Piaggio's own definition of the Vespa as a "two-wheeled small car" deliberately associated it with the world of the automobile. The load-bearing structure proved to be exceptionally robust and far stiffer than a tubular frame of the same weight. Below the monocoque was a tubular swinging arm supporting the engine-wheel assembly. A pair of rubber bump-stops provided a minimal springing effect. The engine cover was attached via clasps and could be removed to access the power unit. The left-hand side-panel was fixed but had a hatch giving access to the interior and allowing it to be used to carry small objects. The 98 model was particularly spartan, lacking any form of rear suspension, while at the front there was a simple ribbon spring. It was not even fitted with a stand: when parked the 98 was laid on the running board (having first closed the fuel tap to prevent flooding). The successive 125 was slightly more comfortable. The front suspension was switched to the right-hand side and featured a more effective coil spring combined with an hydraulic damper. The new rear suspension was also composed

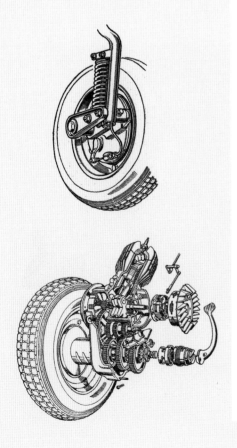

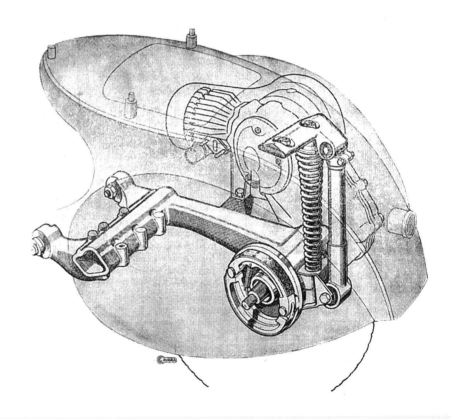

Technical and styling evolution

of a coil spring and hydraulic damper. The single arm struts with cantilevered wheels rather than forks were of clearly aeronautical origin. Contrary to popular belief, the Vespa's wheels were not actually offset to compensate for the engine located on the right-hand side. However, the front wheel was set with a camber angle of 1.5°.

Styling

The engine cover of the 98 had an aperture in line with the cooling fan. The handlebar was tubular, with the headlight mounted on the mudguard. The gearshift rods ran outside the central tunnel. The front mudguard of the first series was particularly deep and had removable walls, while in the second series the mudguard was fixed (and less deep). The round rear light was to remain virtually unchanged throughout the 1940s.

The engine cover of the 125 retained the aperture in line with the cooling fan. The handlebar was tubular and the headlight was mounted on the mudguard. During its production run the 125 benefited from the introduction of a side-stand (instead of being leant on one side like the 98) and then a proper centre stand. The gearshift mechanism also evolved with the rods being run through the centre tunnel before a mixed system of rods and flexible cables was adopted.

PORTA BAGAGLI

SELLINO POSTERIORE

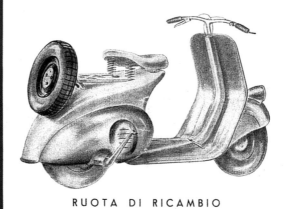

RUOTA DI RICAMBIO

Ditta Giuseppe Lang · Genova

CARRELLO DI RIMORCHIO

The '50s

Engine

The 98 cc displacement was dropped with production concentrating on the classic 125 cc cylinder capacity. In the mid-Fifties, this unit was flanked by the 150 version. With respect to the first generation, the power output was increased slightly: the 125 now gave 5 hp and the 150 5.5 hp. The induction system was modified, with the old three-port and deflector piston configuration being replaced with a cross-flow system with two opposing ports and a flat piston. The gearshift system was significantly improved. The rigid control rods or "bacchette" fitted to the early models were subject to excessive play and required continuous adjustment. In the 1950s gears were selected via far more efficient flexible cables that permitted much greater precision. The GS version of the 150 had a maximum power output of 8 hp and provided significantly improved performance: its maximum speed of 100 kph began to rival that of many motorcycles of the period. One important innovation was the relocation of the carburettor directly above the cylinder. The gearbox was also new and for the first time offered four speeds. The highest specific power output was actually provided by the Sei Giorni version with 7 hp from 125 cc, but this extremely expensive machine was designed specifically for competition.

Technical and styling evolution

Frame,
suspension,
brakes and
wheels

The steel bodywork made the Vespa instantly distinguishable among the various rivals that were beginning to crowd the market. In various areas, however, the monocoque was nonetheless reinforced, above all in the central section. The original aluminium side-panels were replaced with cheaper steel panels with the 1955 version of the 125. The hinged hatch giving access to the carburettor housing remained in the curved centre section of the frame. The presence of hydraulic dampers on both the front and rear suspension helped to improve roadholding as performance levels rose. In order to improve comfort the handlebar was mounted on a cushioned support. The wheels were interchangeable and retained the 8" diameter and consequently the brake drums were also unchanged and began to be somewhat undersized and inefficient in critical situations. The GS version represented significant progress as along with the uprated engine it boasted an improved chassis specification. The suspension featured biconical variable rate springs and dual-acting hydraulic dampers. The diameter of the wheels was increased to 10". The brakes were also improved, with self-ventilating drums to prevent overheating.

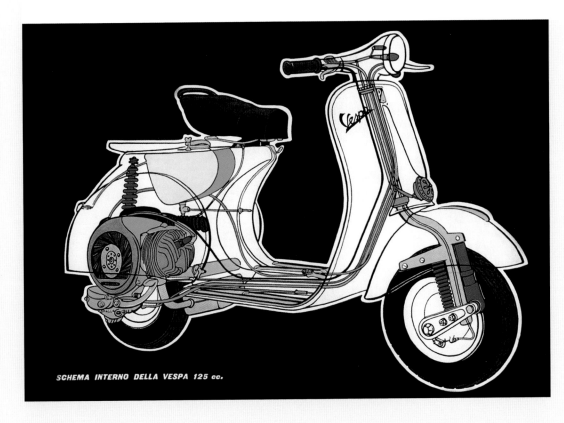

SCHEMA INTERNO DELLA VESPA 125 cc.

Technical and styling evolution

Styling

In the early Fifties the Vespa was still being fitted with a tubular handlebar and a headlight mounted on the mudguard. From 1953, a full engine cover was fitted with no aperture in correspondence with the cooling fan and the styling thus became more uniform. The control cables were external. The only model that was significantly different was the U, the first Vespa with a high, handlebar-mounted headlight. In reality, there was very little special about this version, the U standing for Utilitaria and the fittings reduced to the bare bones to save costs: the bodywork even featured the open engine cover and a cutaway mudguard. The saddle lacked a front spring and the platform lacked rubber strips.

The styling was enhanced and the lines became sleeker in the second half of the Fifties. The left-hand side-panel featured a hatch giving access to the interior. The cables were routed inside the handlebar, providing cleaner lines. The leg-shield still lacked the metal edge trim. The platform was fitted with rubber strips only and the raised portion lacked the rubber mat. A long two-seater saddle was fitted as standard for the first time on the GS. The hatch on the inside part of the monocoque was eliminated in 1957.

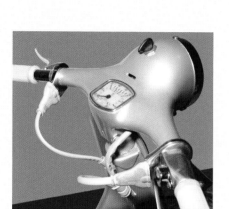

Technical and styling evolution

The '60s

Engine

The '60s saw the introduction of the new 50 cc displacement expressly designed for fourteen-year-olds. Despite having the restricted performance imposed by the Italian Highway Code (a maximum power output of just 1.5 hp) it proved to be an enormous success. Its single cylinder was inclined at 45° rather than being horizontal. There were also innovations in terms of the other displacements. The classic 125 and 150 versions were flanked by the 90 and the 160. Towards the end of the decade the maximum cylinder capacity rose to 180 cc and the engine was subjected to constant development. Thanks to the new induction system the oil-fuel mixture was sprayed directly onto the con-rod assembly, lubricating the bearings. The intake port was located on the crankcase and regulated by the left-hand counterweight of the crankshaft. The first version to adopt this system was the 150 presented in 1958 (it was fitted to the 125 the following year). This important innovation provided numerous advantages in terms of the fuel and lubrication systems, with the possibility of passing from a 5% to a 2% oil-fuel mixture. The major benefit was that of drastically restricting the amount of smoke produced, with less coking and reduced fuel consumption. The electrical system was uprated to take into account the addition of the stoplight required by the new Italian Highway Code. The power output rose constantly and reached a maximum of 10 hp in the 180 Rally, which also boasted the new rotary valve engine.

The engine-gearbox assembly of the Vespa 90 (7.2 hp), top left. Left, a cutaway of the   *Vespa 160 GS engine (8.2 hp). Below, a longitudinal sectional view of the model.*

Technical and styling evolution

Frame,
suspension,
brakes and
wheels

The new 50 presented an interesting new bodywork variation: it was, in fact, the first model to feature fixed rather than removable side-panels. This feature was also adopted on the Nuova 125 that retained the small frame in virtually unaltered form. Access to the engine was gained via a hatch opening transversally via a pair of hinges.

The side-panels were instead removable on all the other larger models. The frame was nonetheless innovative in that it was assembled from two half-shells in sheet metal that were welded together with a central reinforcement. In the GS series, a hatch was let into the rear part giving access to a small locker. However, this was not a practical arrangement and the successive model instead featured the more convenient and capacious glovebox located behind the leg-shield. The last series to use the now obsolete 8" wheels was the 150 Super, all the other models now being fitted with 10" wheels with a view to achieving greater stability.

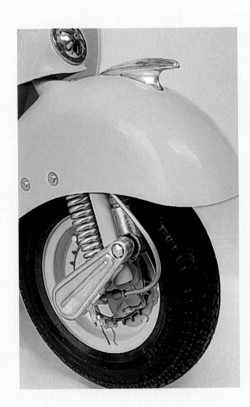

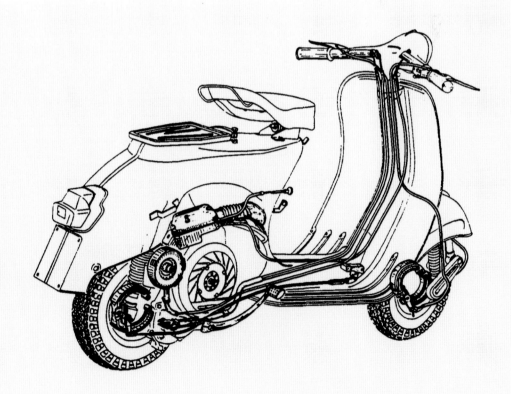

Technical and styling evolution

Styling

An option was introduced for the first time that would be a constant feature of the Vespa range: the doubling up of the monocoque in small and large frame forms. The 125 displacement was unique in that it was found in both categories. In these years the small frame models boasted more up-to-date styling: the side-panels were fixed and well integrated with the principal structure. The 50 and 125 were light and responsive. The 90 was less successful, although the model's reputation was saved by the Super Sprint version that was the dream machine of many enthusiasts. It boasted particularly sleek styling, with a shapelier leg-shield and a lighter front mudguard. Even the handlebar was narrower. The spare wheel was positioned vertically in the centre of the platform with a glovebox mounted on top of it that resembled a motorcycle fuel tank and could be gripped between the knees when riding fast. It even had a chest pad for when you were really tucked in and looking for maximum speed. The 90 SS was also equipped with another component that was eagerly sought after by enthusiasts: that elongated silencer promising ultimate performance that was very different to the "tea kettle" fitted to the other versions with the same frame.

Technical and styling evolution

The large frame models were not ageing so well and suffered to some extent from the dated styling. They were frequently characterised by chromed trim on the side-panels and mudguard, but soon began to reflect the passing of the years. The chromed trim around the edge of the leg-shield was attractive. The headset of the early models was still the type composed of two half-shells, the one-piece unit being adopted later. The rounded tail became more square-cut from 1963 when a registration plate holder was incorporated. The most attractive model remained the Vespa GL, the first to boast the four-speed gearbox, the 2% oil-fuel mixture and the 10" wheels. These are all details still found on the PX of the third millennium, 40 years later… It was also the only model to boast wheels and brake drums in the same colour as the bodywork. In the late Sixties, the 180 SS could boast a well-proportioned design with slightly sharped lines, as you can see in the mudguard and side-panels. One important detail was the capacious glovebox placed behind the leg-shield, a feature destined to last many years. The lively colours such as bright red helped make the 180 SS particularly attractive in the eyes of many enthusiasts.

The '70s

Engine

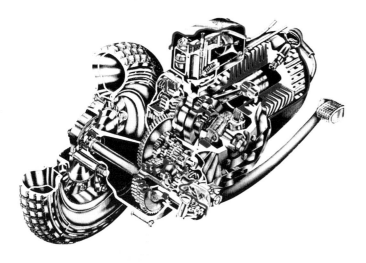

The decade saw the introduction of numerous modifications, from the smallest displacement up. The 50 was in fact offered in the Elestart version, which as the name suggests boasted the sophistication of electric starting. Even though in these years the feature was frowned upon, it was without doubt interesting and well ahead of its time. Apart from the higher cost, the disadvantages consisted of the greater weight and size of the batteries located behind the left-hand side-panel: the weight increased by 11 kg and the spare wheel had to be eliminated. An interesting device controlling lubrication was fitted to the 125 and 150 models. It was offered from the end of the previous decade, initially only on those models reserved for export to markets where there was a lack of facilities for the correct oil-fuel mixtures (as in the USA for example). This was the "Automatic Fuelmix", in effect an automatic premixer providing variable percentages and offered as an optional extra (L. 20,000). The sporty 125 ET3 from 1976 featured three-port induction. The maximum displacement rose to 200 cc in 1972; this represented the largest engine ever fitted to a Vespa and was to remain so for no less than 35 years. The 200 Rally was also the most powerful and fastest ever produced: the engine produced 12.5 hp and was good for a maximum speed of over 115 kph. The 200 also boasted another important innovation, as it was the first Vespa to be fitted with electronic ignition.

Technical and styling evolution

Frame, suspension, brakes and wheels

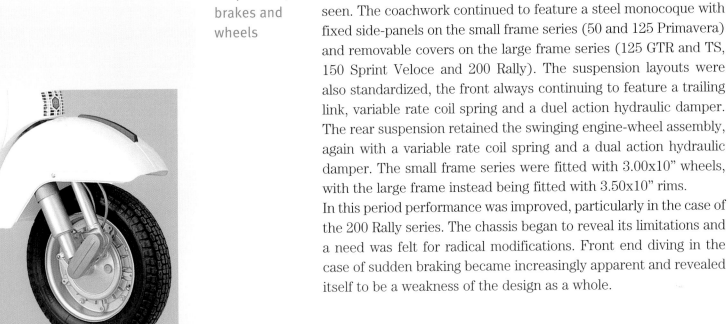

The Vespa frame evolved very little in this decade with the design having becoming a classic and no need for significant changes being seen. The coachwork continued to feature a steel monocoque with fixed side-panels on the small frame series (50 and 125 Primavera) and removable covers on the large frame series (125 GTR and TS, 150 Sprint Veloce and 200 Rally). The suspension layouts were also standardized, the front always continuing to feature a trailing link, variable rate coil spring and a duel action hydraulic damper. The rear suspension retained the swinging engine-wheel assembly, again with a variable rate coil spring and a dual action hydraulic damper. The small frame series were fitted with 3.00x10" wheels, with the large frame instead being fitted with 3.50x10" rims.

In this period performance was improved, particularly in the case of the 200 Rally series. The chassis began to reveal its limitations and a need was felt for radical modifications. Front end diving in the case of sudden braking became increasingly apparent and revealed itself to be a weakness of the design as a whole.

Technical and styling evolution

Styling

The small and large frame series were slightly diversified. The small frame series enjoyed great success, particularly among the younger generations. The fourteen-year-olds loved the 50 Special, the sixteen-year-olds were dazzled by the 125 Primavera. Both models had sleek lines that appealed to the youngsters. A lively range of colours was offered, including audacious tints such as bright green and orange. In order to modernize the appearance of the scooter, the diagonal scripts identical to those of the 98 from 1946 were soon set horizontally and more up-to-date graphics were adopted. There were also new graphics elsewhere on the bodywork, such as the longitudinal stripes applied to Primavera ET3 to emphasize its sporting aspect. The ET3 also featured a matte black elongated exhaust similar to that of the 90 SS from the '60s.

Technical and styling evolution

In terms of styling, the large frame series were a little more subdued. Despite the same displacement, the 125, initially offered as the GTR and then as the TS, was not received by the Piaggio's younger clientele with the same enthusiasm reserved for the Primavera, compared with which it lacked both appeal and performance. The 200 Rally was in a class of its own; it was the fastest Vespa and announced the fact with its longitudinal stripes and the "Electronic" script drawing attention to the ignition system. The 150 Sprint Veloce was in effect better balanced, but was located in what had become a largely ignored category.

With the same displacement, the 125 GTR and TS could not compete with the slim-line Primavera and both were given scant consideration by the teenage market.

The image of the large-frame models began to feel the weight of the passing years and was overly reliant on dated styling. The 200 Rally was a case apart and highly prized by the younger clientele for its uncompromised sporting look. Those longitudinal "racing" stripes may have put off the adults but they certainly appealed to the kids. The motif of contrasting longitudinal bands was not one that was to be revived over the following decades.

The '80s

Engine

In this decade the revolution was more concerned with styling than mechanical aspects, with the engines substantially retaining the characteristics of the corresponding displacements in the previous series. The new PX 125 and 200, for example, had maximum power outputs of 8 and 12.5 hp respectively, the same as those of the TS and the Rally they replaced. The performance figures also coincided.

Separate lubrication had now been extended throughout the range. The PX 125 T5 series broke the mould in that it featured a five-port engine producing a healthy 11 hp. While the situation was relatively stable in terms of the large frame series, there was much more going on among the small frame series. Here too, the power outputs and performance of the PK 50 and 125 remained close to those of the earlier 50 Special and 125 Primavera ET3, but there was one highly important innovation (a veritable revolution in fact) in the transmission department. For the first time, the traditional version with the gripshift gear change was flanked by a new series with an automatic gearbox. The system involved the use of expanding pulleys together with a belt drive to provide continuously variable ratios. The system was fairly sophisticated and was governed by the throttle opening and road speed (via an hydraulic servo mechanism). Although the design was effective it was over-complicated.

Technical and styling evolution

Frame, suspension, brakes and wheels

The bodywork of the new series, while being thoroughly revised in stylistic terms, retained the original steel monocoque in unaltered form. Another aspect that was left unchanged was the size of the wheels, now established at 3.50x10". The suspension department, one long in need of development, was instead thoroughly revised. The performance of the last models was capable of seriously embarrassing the front suspension, especially in the case of sudden braking. The front geometry was therefore completely revised, albeit without straying far from the general configuration previously adopted. The damper was anchored to the brake backplate and attached to the trailing link in correspondence with the stub axle. In this way the notorious nose-diving effect under braking was considerably reduced and roadholding was significantly improved. Thanks to these improvements, the Vespa was once more an up-to-date vehicle and, above all, well balanced in relation to its new performance potential. From this point of view, the greatest benefit was felt by the 200 version, the most powerful scooter on the market.

Technical and styling evolution

Styling

There was a clearly differentiated public response to the small and large frame series. The PK series was intended to replace the previous models (the 50 Special and the 125 Primavera) but failed dismally. Compared with the corresponding models from the '70s the styling was excessively square-cut and had nothing like the same appeal. An attempt was made to repair the damage with the launch of the PK XL series, but in styling terms it only made matters worse with its conspicuous saddle support that was ill at ease with the rest of the body. Among the technical details, mention should be made of the internal rather than overlapping bodywork welds. The Automatica was the first Vespa not to feature a foot brake (replaced by the left-hand headset lever).

The sports series was called the ETS and had longitudinal bands and an elongated exhaust like that of the ET3 from the '70s. The only feature that was truly appreciated in terms of the styling of the small frame series was the fact that the indicators were now incorporated within the leg-shield and at the rear end of the two side-panels. This provided much more modern lines compared with the previous series and represents a styling detail worthy of note.

Technical and styling evolution

The large frame was instead a remarkable success. From the very outset the PX proved to be a masterpiece, demonstrated by the fact that it is still virtually unchanged and selling strongly well into the third millennium. Its presentation represented an epochal moment for Piaggio. Compared with the '70s generation everything changed and there was the risk of alienating a large section of the public. Instead the PX retained all the qualities of the previous models, but was revised and improved in every respect. It was also updated; indicators perfectly integrated with the bodywork were offered as optional extras and proved to be so popular that examples without them are rare.

There was also a more sporting version, the T5. It was more powerful and faster but stylistically flawed, with an ugly rectangular headlight. It was also over-styled: there was even a spoiler below the platform!

The front end of the pre-production examples of the PX tended to float, provoking excessive wallowing. In order to correct this problem, the scooter was taken to the Fiat wind tunnel for aerodynamic testing.

The '90s

Engine

In this decade too there were no major changes to the power unit, the revolution being largely aesthetic. The engine retained what were now the three classic displacements, 125, 150 and 200 cc. The maximum power outputs were also unchanged with respect to the PX series with the same displacements: 8, 9 and 12 hp respectively. The same was true of the various models' performance, with the figures close to those for the corresponding models from the '70s. Modifications were minimal: the ports were larger, the sparkplug was located more centrally and the cylinder head had a truncated cone configuration. Compared with the preceding models the choke and fuel tap controls were eliminated in favour of automatic devices. One enriched the oil/fuel mixture in relation to the ambient temperature (and closed automatically), the other closed the flow of fuel with the engine switched off and engaged the reserve supply, signalled via a tell-tale on the headset. The engine mounts consisted of larger flexible supports in order to further reduce the transmission of vibration. In the small frame series the only significant interventions concerned the automatic transmission that was simplified with respect to the first version, with the new Speedmatic system featuring a mechanical rather than hydraulic variator.

The Vespa Bimodale

The prototype Vespa 50 Bimodale was presented at the Cologne Show in 1990. It was equipped with a dual power unit: a classic internal combustion two-stroke engine and an electric motor. The batteries were located in the left-hand frame compartment and were charged by the internal combustion engine. The scooter had a maximum speed of 25 kph and a range of 15 km. This was an extremely interesting one-off experimental vehicle that never made it past the prototype stage.

The Bimodale was primarily an experimental vehicle designed to be ridden on all roads with the normal internal combustion engine while the electric motor could be used in urban areas without polluting the air with exhaust gases. The experiment was later repeated with the Sfera model.

Technical and styling evolution

Frame,
suspension,
brakes and
wheels

The Cosa bodywork was all new and realized in Xenoil, a plastic material that once painted had an identical finish to the metal bodies. The frame, suspension and brakes package represent a clear advance in terms of safety. In particular, the designers focussed on the braking system in order to offer greater efficiency with respect to the previous generations. The Cosa was equipped with an integral braking system. This means that by depressing the pedal an hydraulic control is actuated that acts on both drums, automatically differentiating the braking force applied to the front and rear wheels. The handlebar lever instead actuated the front brake only, but when the pedal was already in action it did not increase braking force so as to avoid the risk of locking the front wheel. The hydraulic pump was located inside the central tunnel, close to the pedal and distributed braking force between the two units via a valve, giving priority to the rear wheel. ABS was available as an optional extra. With the Cosa, comfort was further improved thanks to more effective suspension, while wider tyres were fitted to increase stability. For the first time there was a space beneath the saddle to stow a helmet.

Technical and styling evolution

Styling

The small and large frame series were significantly diversified. The small frame was improved while the large frame suffered something of a disaster. With regard to the N and the FL2, Piaggio took steps to soften the excessively angular styling of the PK from the previous decade. While they were by no means masterpieces, they did begin to be accepted by the public.

The steering shroud was integrated more effectively with the front mudguard, the headset was better shaped in the area adjacent to the grips, the instrumentation was clearer and more comprehensive and the glovebox was more smoothly integrated with the back of the leg-shield. In the version with automatic transmission the lateral vents on the side-panels were eliminated. The plastic wheel covers were also more attractive (although rather impractical when the tyres had to be inflated).

The improvement with respect to the small frame models from the previous decade was significant. The larger instrumentation was particularly popular. For the first time the Vespa 50 was also fitted with a truly legible speedometer and well-positioned tell-tale lights; furthermore, there was also the luxury of a fuel gauge.

Technical and styling evolution

It was instead with the large frame that Piaggio made a major mistake in attempting to replace a "perfect" model, the PX. It was objectively difficult to improve on the styling of a masterpiece, but with the Cosa the firm managed quite the opposite. Then there was the fact that abandoning the Vespa name was a strategic decision that smacked of commercial masochism.

The styling of the Cosa paid great attention to the placing of the indicators within the bodywork; those at the front were angular and inset, while those at the rear formed a band that included the rear light in the centre. The result was harmonious and met with public approval.

The Cosa 2 was decidedly less successful and was penalised by the over-styled rear end. In this case, the registration plate was inserted between the two indicators with the rear light being squashed below the saddle creating a visual impact that upset and interfered with the lines of the tail. The Cosa seemed to do everything it could to make itself unpopular.

The 2000s

Engine

Major innovations for the small frame series: the birth of the 125 ET4 (an evolution of the LX) and the fitting of a four-stroke engine to the Vespa for the first time. This was not an absolute first for Piaggio: the technology had already been seen on the Sfera 125, but here modifications were made to the carburettor, the exhaust system and the ignition electronics. The engine also featured an overhead camshaft and an oil radiator cooled by the same flow of air cooling the cylinder barrel. The transmission was automatic, but of a simpler and more efficient design than that of the PK series. There was also exceptional changes to the smallest displacement model with the birth of the 50 ET2 powered by a two-stroke engine fitted with a sophisticated direct fuel injection system. Ten years on, the large frame system also evolved with the Granturismo model. This series featured liquid cooling with the radiator air intake concealed either side of the glovebox behind the leg-shield. The classic 125 and 200 displacements (the 150 was dropped) were later joined by the 250, the first time a Vespa displacement had ever exceeded 200 cc, 35 years after the introduction of the Rally. Power outputs and performance figures were improved, with no less than 22 hp propelling the scooter to a maximum speed of over 120 kph. The engine is extremely advanced: four-stroke, four valves, electronic fuel injection and ignition. The Vespa Granturismo was the first 250 in Europe homologated in accordance with the Euro 3 anti-smog norms.

Hybrid, an ecological Vespa

The world's first hybrid two-wheeler!
In the spring of 2006 Piaggio presented the Municipality of Milan with the first example of the Vespa 50 LX bimodale, a development of the model introduced at the 1990 Cologne Show. This prototype, designated as the HyS (Hybrid Scooter), is effectively equipped with two power units, an internal combustion engine and an electric motor. The first is a classic catalyzed four-stroke, while the second instead turns the LX into a zero emissions vehicle able to circulate in city centres even when the level of atmospheric pollution leads to a ban on vehicles with internal combustion engines. A switch permits the selection of one of four operating modes: standard hybrid, high charge, low charge and electric only. In the first three, power is derived from both units (for example, the electric motor can give the internal combustion a boost when climbing) thanks to an integrated system, while in the last the internal combustion engine is disengaged.

What is innovative is that when it is running the internal combustion engine is charging the electric motor's batteries. The differences with respect to the standard LX can be seen beneath the saddle with the compartment of the HyS occupied by the batteries: a top box has to be used to store a helmet.

Technical and styling evolution

Frame,
suspension,
brakes and
wheels

The Granturismo large frame series revived the steel monocoque frame with welded reinforcements. The side-panels are fixed. The front suspension has a single-strut layout with a twin-chamber hydraulic damper and coaxial spring. The rear suspension has a pair of dual-action dampers with adjustable preloading. For the first time a Vespa was fitted with 12" diameter wheels. ABS was offered as an optional extra along with an integral braking system: the left-hand lever actuates both brakes, while the right-hand lever acts exclusively on the front disc. The braking system is servo-assisted. The discs have a diameter of no less than 220 mm.

In the small frame series, the LX was fitted with 11" wheels of a new five-spoke design. In this period the question of active safety became increasingly important. While until then all models had been fitted with 10" diameter wheels, a significant increase in this dimension was introduced that provided greater stability on rough or loosely surfaced roads.

Technical and styling evolution

Styling

Moving into the new millennium with an all-new design, albeit one carrying the Vespa name, was always going to be a difficult task. With the benefit of the experience gained during the previous decades, Piaggio knew it was facing a terrible risk. In the 1970s everything had gone well for the firm, while in the '80s the large frame was extremely popular but the small frame failed to find favour. The '90s instead saw the resurgence of the small frame and the decline of the large frame.

The world waited for Piaggio's 50th anniversary celebrations with bated breath: when the covers were removed a small frame scooter was revealed. This was the ET4 and toasts were made to both the anniversary and the beauty of the new model. It was so popular that in the middle of the following decade it was replaced by the LX series with only a few details having been revised. These included the headlight, with a round unit once again preferred to the oval version in a clear reference to the past. The small frame series proved to be a great success in terms of its perfectly balanced styling and details. The tapering side-panels were particularly popular and successfully rendered the idea of a dynamic vehicle. A small design masterpiece.

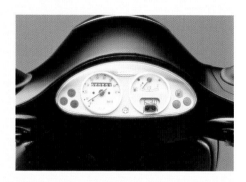

Technical and styling evolution

The public waited impatiently for the large frame – this was the first time that the two series were not produced in parallel. However, Piaggio wanted to be sure of offering a successful large Vespa and delayed for no less than ten years. It was worth the wait, with the new Granturismo proving to be hugely popular.

The design is extremely up-to-date and skilfully manages to reference many stylistic elements that have contributed to the success of the Vespa over the years. For example, the script on the leg-shield is set diagonally and the Piaggio badge is the two-tone version, while the headlight is set off by a chromed bezel. For the first time, the liquid cooling posed the problem of where to locate air vents. The designers took advantage of the sides of the glovebox mounted behind the leg-shield to house modern features without disturbing the deliberately classical styling.

Another feature that has proved to be very popular is the incorporation of the passenger footrests within the body when they are folded. The luggage rack behind the saddle is useful, practical and sturdy. A body-coloured top box is also available for those looking for extra carrying capacity.

The 2010s

Engine

In 2012, the Engineering Department at Pontedera began work on a true masterpiece: the 3V engine. The name identifies the three valves, the fruit of a lengthy series of studies conducted over the previous years. The objective that had been set was particularly ambitious: maintaining the same power output of the engines hitherto used while reducing fuel consumption by 30%. A truly demanding challenge, even for a colossus such as Piaggio. The engineers focussed on the 125 and 150 cc displacements fitted to the small frame series and showed their expertise in achieving a significant result: this was the beginning of a new generation of engines. The new 3V was actually born against the tide in the sense that it has a long stroke, a choice made to ensure good breathing and reduce consumption. Compared with the earlier engines, the power output was increased by a single horsepower at the same rev speed. The three valves represent an excellent compromise between the preceding two and the four that would guarantee improved performance. Of the three valves, two are reserved for the intake system. In the new design, modifications have also been made to the manifolds so as to guarantee maximum efficiency with regard to the turbulence of the fuel air mixture. The forced-air cooling system was also revised and above all attention was paid to reducing friction with the crankshaft mounted on plain bearings, the camshaft on ball bearings and the rockers on roller bearings.

Technical and styling evolution

The running gear

The new 3V engines initially equipped the small frame models in the LX and S series that retained virtually unchanged the running gear used by the earlier 2V models.

What was much more obvious was the technical-stylistic revision of the new small frame models built from 2014. These replaced the earlier versions and were named as the Primavera and the Sprint.

The monocoque of the new series was completely redesigned and on this occasion a new swinging engine mounting system was introduced that uses bearings rather than rubber buffers. The damper and front suspension mounts were also repositioned. These changes contributed to a significant improvement in running stability and a major reduction in the vibration transmitted to the rider.

In order to lower the centre of gravity, the battery was located lower, in the longitudinal member, giving rise to a layout that also allowed the capacity of the bay underneath the saddle to be increased. The front brake was also modified with a new floating caliper with a pair of side-by-side rather than stacked pistons. The chassis retained the previous pressed steel monocoque structure albeit in revised form to guarantee increased stiffness for the same weight.

Technical and styling evolution

Styling

In this decade, the small frame series was the first to be subjected to a restyling operation, launched with the Primavera, a historical reference to one of the best-loved models in Vespa history. Light and pacey, adored by the young, the original had enjoyed great success thanks in part to its perfectly judged styling. The new Primavera lives up to the standards set by its predecessor thanks to particularly successful styling characterised by a new rounded and raised headlight. The lines of the leg-shield are very clean, enhanced by a chromed border and a new and particularly slim and streamlined grille. Numerous aspects were improved with respect to the earlier LX series, with a reduction in the number of plastic components and greater attention being paid to detailing. For example, both the mixed digital-analogue instrumentation and the handlebar controls are new. The indicators feature LEDs with a daytime running function (DRL). The platform has rubber ribbing and chrome trim. A great deal of attention has been paid to the rear section, characterised by light, tapering lines that emphasise the slim and agile look. The contemporary Sprint version is instead distinguished by the trapezoidal shape of the headlight and the new wheels with 12" rims. From the second half of the decade, numerous modifications were also made to the large frame series.

Technical and styling evolution

The 946 series is a case apart. This is a truly special model offered at a truly special price. Presented at Eicma in Milan in 2012 it went into production the following year. What might initially have been seen as a kind of "provocation" to be displayed on the Piaggio show stand was instead a very concrete proposal from the Styling Centre at Pontedera. The designers were interested in evaluating the impact of the "Vespa of the future". Conjugating past and future was an enormous responsibility and an incredibly difficult task. The designers actually went right back to the forebear of the first Vespa: the MP6 prototype that cuts a fine figure in the Pontedera museum. Like the original, the new 946 boasts a "spine" with extremely clean lines and a suspended saddle: a feature achieved thanks to an elegant and sophisticated aluminium casting. Another clear reference to the prototype came in the form of the slots on the tail, introduced to guarantee adequate cooling. Among the problems tackled was the by no means easy positioning of the single rear damper, located horizontally for the first time while respecting the tapering lines imposed by the stylists. The 946, there is no lack of dedicated accessories such as a luggage rack, a case matching the saddle and a helmet.

In 2015, an even more exclusive version of the 946 was presented, the Emporio Armani. This is a model expressly dedicated to the celebrated stylist and characterised by a special livery of grey with subtle hints of green.

Part three

ORIGIN AND DEVELOPMENT

The forerunners

The prototypes

In the late '30s and early '40s four vehicles were built in Italy that represent the nation's first attempts at building a scooter, a vehicle with two small wheels: the Fiat, the Volugrafo, the Delta and the Simat. None of them actually made it into production, in part due to the rather basic, albeit fully finished, configuration of the projects. Other scooters had already gone into production abroad, but none had achieved commercial success. The most interesting models appeared in the Twenties in France (Monet Goyon), Germany (Lomos), Great Britain (Unibus) and the United States (Autoped). A number of models from the USA achieved moderate success in the Thirties (Cushman, Motoscoot, Salsbury).

Fiat, 1938

This was effectively the first Italian scooter. Built as a one-off, it was registered as being owned by Giancarlo Camerana, then Vice President of Fiat. At the time Camerana was a close friend of Enrico Piaggio.
The scooter was powered by a Type 32 Sachs two-stroke engine displacing 98 cc. It produced a power output of 2 hp and ran on a 6% fuel/oil mixture. The two-speed gearbox was controlled by hand via a lever. The front suspension was composed of a semi-elliptic spring linked to a system of struts. The rear suspension was rigid. Lateral drum brakes were fitted along with 8" wheels.

The forerunners

Volugrafo,
1939

Designed by the engineer Vittorio Belmondo, this basic scooter was built by Aermoto of Turin.

It was also powered by a Type 32 Sachs two-stroke engine displacing 98 cc. It produced a power output of 2 hp and ran on a 6% fuel/oil mixture. The two-speed gearbox was controlled via a central lever. Both front and rear suspension was rigid. Drum brakes were fitted with 8" wheels. The scooter weighed 58 kg. There was also a version with a displacement of 124 cc.

The Volugrafo was a particularly interesting model and boasted a number of engineering features that were to have a future in the commercial development of the scooter such as small diameter wheels – this provided excellent manoeuvrability, but a spare wheel was not offered. The opening hatch in the side accessing the engine was to be copied faithfully on the prototype MP5 Paperino built by Piaggio in 1944.

The Volugrafo was conceptually spartan; it was neither comfortable to ride nor practical given the inconvenient positioning of the gear lever. There was no stand which meant that when parked it had to be leant with one running board on the ground. The colour scheme was very eye-catching with all components painted in bright red.

The forerunners

Simat, 1940

This scooter was virtually identical to the Volugrafo. It too was designed by Vittorio Belmondo who intended to market it himself and was again powered by a 98 cc Sachs two-stroke engine. The steel bodywork was pressed in a single piece. The running boards served as footrests but also as something to lean the vehicle on when parked given that it lacked a stand. The running boards were in aluminium. As with the Volugrafo, comfort was at a premium given that the Simat had no suspension other than the pair of springs set below the saddle. The fuel filler cap was placed behind the saddle. The wheels were fitted with spinners for rapid removal, an understandable feature given the frequency with which in those years tyres had to be repaired due to punctures; despite their small diameter, a spare wheel was not provided.

Compared with the Volugrafo from the previous year, the body-shell was distinguished by a conspicuous hump beneath the saddle. The front mudguard also extended further forward than that of the Volugrafo.

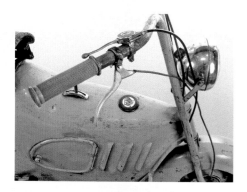

The forerunners

Velta, 1941

The Velta was yet another design by Vittorio Belmondo. It was actually an improved version of the Simat, now equipped with front suspension and powered by the customary a 98 cc Sachs two-stroke engine.

The Velta represents the final evolutionary stage of the scooter conceived by Belmondo. The bodyshell was identical to that of the earlier Simat, from which it also inherited the inconvenient gear lever location virtually in the centre of the body.

The presence of front suspension capable of providing a modicum of ride comfort instead represented significant progress. The layout featured a pair of coil springs located either side of the steering head, a configuration similar to that adopted in the same period on the far larger Harley Davidsons built in the United States.

In contrast with earlier prototype models by the same designer, the Velta features extensive use of the VBT initials standing for Vittorio Belmondo Torino. The initials are found all over the scooter, almost obsessively, from the front suspension struts to the handlebar levers.

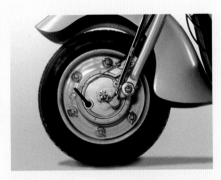

The forerunners

MP5
Moto Piaggio
Paperino, 1944

In order to escape the bombing of Pontedera, Piaggio moved to Biella. Here the engineers Renzo Spolti and Vittorio Casini had the opportunity to admire the collection of motorcycles found in the castle of a great enthusiast, Count Felice Trossi. Among the various models, one in particular attracted their attention, Vittorio Belmondo's Volugrafo. With inspiration being drawn from this model, the first example of what was to be the forerunner of the Vespa was built by Piaggio: the MP5, or Moto Piaggio 5, also known as the Paperino (Donald Duck) following on from the Fiat Topolino (Mickey Mouse). The entire project was realised within the experimental department. Only the engine (Sachs 98) and the tyres (Superga) were outsourced.

The Paperino had a number of interesting features: the voluminous bodywork, the handlebar controls, forced-air cooling and small-diameter wheels. However, the central tunnel had to be straddled to mount the scooter, something that did not please Enrico Piaggio. It was sufficient for production of the Paperino to be restricted to just a few dozen examples.

Following the Paperino episode, Enrico Piaggio decided to entrust the project to the engineer Corradino D'Ascanio who was responsible for the prototype of what was to become the first Vespa model, the 98.

The forerunners

The forerunners

MP6
Moto Piaggio,
1945

This prototype was so successful that the Vespa that went into production was virtually identical. The only difference lay in the type of cooling: natural ventilation in the prototype and forced air in the production model. The prototype was, in fact, distinguished by large grilles at the front and rear of the engine cover.

A number of features that were to characterize the Vespa from then on were present at the outset. The bodywork was particularly extensive and the mudguards were deep to offer thorough protection and avoid soiling riders' clothes. This aeronautic inspired solution, conceived by D'Ascanio for the front strut, with a single-tube damper and a overhanging wheel instead of the tradinional fork, appeared to be a very unusual combination for a motorcycle. The rear mounted engine allowed the scooter to be mounted easily without having to straddle a central tunnel and kept the engine-transmission assembly compact. The small-diameter wheels guaranteed great manoeuvrability and allowed a spare wheel to be carried. The handlebar controls made the Vespa easy to use for everyone; the concentration of controls on the handlebar, including the gearbox was patended by Piaggio in 1946. Minimal modifications were required for mass production:

The forerunners

the asymmetric side-panels of the prototype became symmetrical and the horn was shifted from under the saddle to the leg-shield. A number of prototypes were constructed, but they may be divided into two series. One version had the brake pedal on the right, angular side-panels (with a lower fold), no badging on the leg-shield, the gear-shift behind the shield part rigid and part flexible and a kick-start pedal with an articulated arm. A second version had the brake pedal on the left, rounded side-panels (with no lower fold), a Piaggio logo in the centre of the leg-shield (or a Vespa script on the left), rigid gearshift controls and a non-jointed kick-start pedal. Development and construction of the first prototypes was very fast: only three months were required to produce the first running MP6.

The prototypes were tested on the Biella-Oropa road by Vittorio Casini, who was to say, in his thick Tuscan accent: «Questo hoso qui ti va anche sui muri» («This thing'll even climb walls»).

Part two

THE ROAD TO SUCCESS

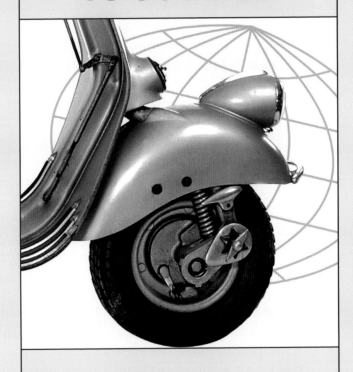

The '40s

The '40s

CINEMA
Citizen Kane (Orson Welles) - *Obsession* (Luchino Visconti) - *Casablanca* (Michael Curtiz) - *Gilda* (Charles Vidor) - *Sciuscià* (Vittorio De Sica)

MUSIC
Tulipan (Trio Lescano) - *White Christmas* (Bing Crosby) - *Nella Vecchia Fattoria* (Quartetto Cetra) - *Latino music - Boogie-Woogie*

RADIO
Radio Londra - Canta Rabagliati - Oggi a Montecitorio - Arcobaleno - La Bisarca - Voci dal mondo - I notturni dell'usignolo - Radio plays

BOOKS
The Tartar Steppe (Buzzati) - *Don Camillo* (Giovannino Guareschi) - *1984* (Orwell) - For Whom the Bell Tolls (Ernest Hemingway)

CARS
Renault 4 CV - Cisitalia - Alfa Romeo 6C 2500 - Citroën 2 CV - Lancia Aprilia - Fiat 500 - Land Rover

MOTORCYCLES
Solex - Ducati Cucciolo - Gilera 500 Saturno - Moto Guzzi 500 Astore - Matchless 500 G80 - Morini 125

FASHION
Nylon stocking production suspended in 1943 and reintroduced in 1947 - Wedge soles - Bikinis - US military T-shirts

INNOVATIONS
Polaroid - Nikon 1 - Penicilin - Sonar - Teflon - Electronic calculator - Dacron textile fiber - Vitamin A

ENTERTAINMENT
Pinball - Vinyl 33/78 records - Car radio - First TV ads in the USA - NTSC standard TV transmissions

SPORT
London Olympics (1948) - Post-war Mille Miglia and Le Mans 24 Hours - Gino Bartali wins Tour de France (1948) - Fausto Coppi wins Giro d'Italia

EVENTS
Second World War - Atomic bombs in Hiroshima and Nagasaki - Birth of Italian Republic (1946) - Marshall Plan aids Europe

The '40s

The diffidence shown towards a vehicle that was so different with respect to those the public was accustomed to was considerable, with the small wheels arousing concern over roadholding. However, those who tried the Vespa were enthusiastic and thanks to word-of-mouth it began to establish a following. Piaggio advertising did the rest and from the 2500 examples produced in 1946, output rose to 61,000 in 1950. There were just two models in those years, the 98 and the 125. The gear change mechanism used the rod system and required a certain degree of maintenance.

The 98 had a power output of 3.3 hp at 4500 rpm and a maximum speed of 60 kph. The gearbox had three speeds. In the 125 the power output rose to 4 hp at 4500 rpm for a maximum speed of 70 kph. The most significant improvement introduced with the 125 was coil spring suspension on both wheels.

Piaggio moved to Biella in 1944. The offices were located in the warehouses of the Poma cotton mill and the Squindo foundry, while the production lines were set up in the textile factories belonging to Faudella at Pavignano, Barberis at Candelo and Pettinatura di Vigliano at Gaglianico and Lessona. The two-tone logo was designed in the immediate post-war period when Enrico Piaggio

In the early years of its career the Vespa presence was felt everywhere, from the great international expositions to local town fairs, ensuring that the message reached the widest possible public.

The '40s

decided to restart production. It is comprises a heraldic-style shield with a pointed tip, divided diagonally. Set in the upper part was a white "P" on a blue ground, while below was a blue Piaggio script on a light blue ground. The Boldoni font used was very traditional for that period.

Vespa,
the story
of a name

Legend has it that Enrico Piaggio's first words when he saw the prototype Vespa were, «It looks like a wasp!». In reality, it is by no means certain that he was actually the first to associate the new scooter with the insect. What is certain is that the name was a success from the outset. There are actually two strands to the scooter-insect correlation. There are those who see in the pinched shape the separation between the head-handlebar and the thorax-body, while others pointed to the similarity of the insect's buzz and that of the scooter.

Fortunately, the virtues of the new scooter were soon recognised by all those who were not motorcyclists but nonetheless wished for a means of individual transport that was simple, economical and – above all – non-sporting.

The advertising campaign involved well-known international personalities. This photo shows *one of the first Vespas being personally presented to a young Prince Rainier of Monaco.*

ANNO XXXII - N.° 7
10 APRILE 1946

Questa copia
Lire Trenta
Sped. in A. Post. Gru 2.

RASSEGNA DELLA PRODUZIONE
MOTOCICLISTICA ITALIANA

Caratteristiche della motoleggera "VESPA": motore a 2 tempi - cilindrata 98 cmc. - velocità massima 60 km. ora - consumo 1 litro per 50 km. - cambio a 3 marce - massima pendenza superabile 20% - sospensione elastica, anteriore e posteriore. Rappresentante per la vendita: S. A. R. P. I. - Genova - Via Galata 33 - Telefono 54770.

Anche la motocicletta appare oggi in una fase nettamente evolutiva e fra le costruzioni italiane del dopoguerra la nuovissima "VESPA" della PIAGGIO & C. di Genova che qui presentiamo costituisce una brillante incarnazione di tendenze profondamente innovatrici ma basate su principi razionali tradotti in concreto con attenta meditazione. I primi esemplari della "VESPA" hanno fornito in pratica eccellenti risultati. La serietà della ditta costruttrice garantisce d'altronde di per se stessa la bontà di questa macchina, la prima che, nella produzione su vasta scala, batta vie decisamente nuove.

The '40s

From the owner's handbook:

- *Gears may also be changed without disengaging the clutch. Exhaustive testing with this system has demonstrated that the transmission components do not suffer.*
- *The Vespa light motorcycle does not have a stand, it may be leant with the running boards directly on the ground or preferably on a kerb. When the motorcycle is leant on the running board the fuel tap should be closed to avoid flooding the carburettor. It is advisable to lean the motorcycle on the left-hand running board.*
- *Clean the exhaust silencer every 4000 km by introducing water and caustic soda (25%) and then rinsing thoroughly with running water.*
- *If the carburettor is flooded when starting the engine, close the fuel tap and drain the fuel from the engine by unscrewing the plug in the lower section of the crankcase. Turn the engine over by hand until the fuel is completely drained, screw in the plug and actuate the starting lever with the fuel tap still closed, reopening the tap as soon as the engine fires.*

The voice of the press

From *Motociclismo*, 10th April 1946:

In the last few days Piaggio & C. of Genoa has presented to the public the "Vespa" utilitarian light motorcycle mass-produced in its Pontedera factory. This machine represents one of the most important aspects of Piaggio's peacetime production programme which must provide work for its major industrial facilities, until recently devoted to the production of munitions, specifically aircraft, aero-engines and variable pitch propellers. Aviators and aviation specialists and technicians have always been enthusiasts of and frequently knowledgeable experts with regard to motorcycles. It should come as no surprise that these engineers, open-minded innovators by necessity and tradition, when invited to design a utilitarian light motorcycle, should have left to one side the classical school and attempted to resolve the problem on the basis of criteria that were their own, if not wholly new or revolutionary.

The practical result has proved more than satisfactory: both manoeuvrability and roadholding are very good, even on fairly rough roads and muddy terrain. The suspension offers excellent ride comfort. The front leg-shield, which to date has no provisions to this end, could be equipped with hooks and rings to carry bags and other objects you never know where to stow on a motorcycle. Overall, you get the impression that the "Vespa" should be favourably received and enjoy considerable success, especially taking into consideration the sale price that, even though it is still fairly high in relation to the reduced purchasing power of the general public, is excellent in comparison with the current prices on our market and reasonably in line with the prices on some foreign markets.

The '40s

Highly sought–after today by all collectors, when it appeared on the market the 98 was by no means as successful as had been hoped. According to a Piaggio report of the period, «the first months of distribution were not encouraging. It was a struggle to sell the first 50 examples produced. It is a year of losses for the group and it does not appear that the investment in the Vespa will bring the forecast results.»

The reason is to be found in traditional motorcyclists' distrust of the "small wheels" and their consequent snubbing of this alternative vehicle. But then, the Vespa was not designed for them. Fortunately, the virtues of the new scooter were rapidly recognised by all those who were not motorcyclists but nonetheless wished for a means of individual transport that was simple, economical and, above all, non-sporting. Thanks in part to the extensive advertising campaign staged at the behest of Enrico Piaggio and the fact that from the outset the firm aimed to conquer a female clientele, the Vespa gradually began to acquire a reputation. However, true success only arrived with the successive 125. The Innocenti Lambretta was born in 1947: it was the beginning of a 30-year-long rivalry.

The voice of the dealers

Testimony: the first dealer: the Fiat-Ghizzoni concessionaire in Milan, Tancredi di Giambattista, owner of the dealership, tells his story:

Ghizzoni had been a Fiat concessionaire since before the war. When Enrico Piaggio asked Osvaldo Ghizzoni whether we were interested in trying a new light motorcycle design, we went straight down to Pontedera. We were the first to be called among all the dealers in Italy, Lombardy was a highly attractive market. It was winter and at Viareggio they had already organized the first carnival. Half the factory was in ruins. There were no windows in the offices, we found Enrico Piaggio with an army blanket over his shoulders.
The Vespa immediately made a... terrible impression on us. They showed it to us in a workshop. It was a prototype. We didn't like it because we were still tied to the image of the motorcycle. It looked like an abortion to us. An engineer, his name was Carbonero, invited me
to have a go in the workshop. And suddenly I changed my mind. The floor was rough, but right away I realized that the Vespa could be a brilliant solution to the problem of personal transport. I realized that it was a very clever vehicle with that handlebar gear changer, the monocoque body, the covered engine, the spare wheel and the opportunity to keep one's legs together.
Via Sarpi in Milan, there was a queue to try the Vespa. The test rides took place in the courtyard. A tester on a ramp in the workshop then demonstrated that the Vespa could also tackle steep slopes. It was a great success. To make sure Fiat wasn't overshadowed, Osvaldo Ghizzoni created an independent, parallel company, "S.A.R.P.I.", again in Via Sarpi in premises close to our own. The Vespa constituted the first true Italian miracle. Capital was in short supply; at times Pontedera would call us because they urgently needed an advance, they lived from day to day...

Part two

THE ROAD TO SUCCESS

The '50s

The '50s

CINEMA
Totò - On the Waterfront (Elia Kazan) - *Poveri ma belli* (Dino Risi) - *I soliti ignoti* (Mario Monicelli) - *Ben Hur* (William Wyler) - *Sabrina* (Billy Wilder)

MUSIC
Rock Around the Clock (Bill Haley) - *Love Me Tender* (Elvis Presley) - *Only You* (The Platters) - *Volare* (Domenico Modugno)

RADIO
First transmissions in Germany and Italy - Lascia o raddoppia - Carosello - Musichiere - Perry Mason - Canzonissima - Rin Tin Tin - Festival di Sanremo

BOOKS
Mondo piccolo (Giovannino Guareschi) - *The Old Man and the Sea* (Ernest Hemingway) - *Il Gattopardo* (Giuseppe Tomasi di Lampedusa)

CARS
Porsche 356 - Lancia Aurelia - Alfa Romeo Giulietta - Ford Thunderbird - Fiat 500/600/1100 - Citroën DS 19

MOTORCYCLES
Ariel 500 Twin - Benelli 125 Leoncino - BSA 500 Gold Star - Gilera 500 Saturno - MV Agusta 125

FASHION
Leather bomber jacket - Pointed bras - Skirts and petticoats - Baby-doll - Stiletto heels - Jeans - Brilliantine - Christian Dior's "New Look"

INNOVATIONS
Television - Jukeboxes - Electric razors - Washing machines - Cinemascope - Transistors - Olivetti Lettera 22 typewriter - Sputnik

ENTERTAINMENT
Hula-hop - Polistil miniature models - Lego - Portable record-player - Comics Tex Willer - Drive-in

SPORT
Coppi wins Giro d'Italia/Tour de France (1952) - Ascari World Champion with Ferrari (1952 and 1953) - Helsinki and Melbourne Olympics

EVENTS
Berlin Iron Curtain - Edmund Hillary climbs Everest (1953) - Revolution in Cuba - Six European countries give rise to the EEC (1957)

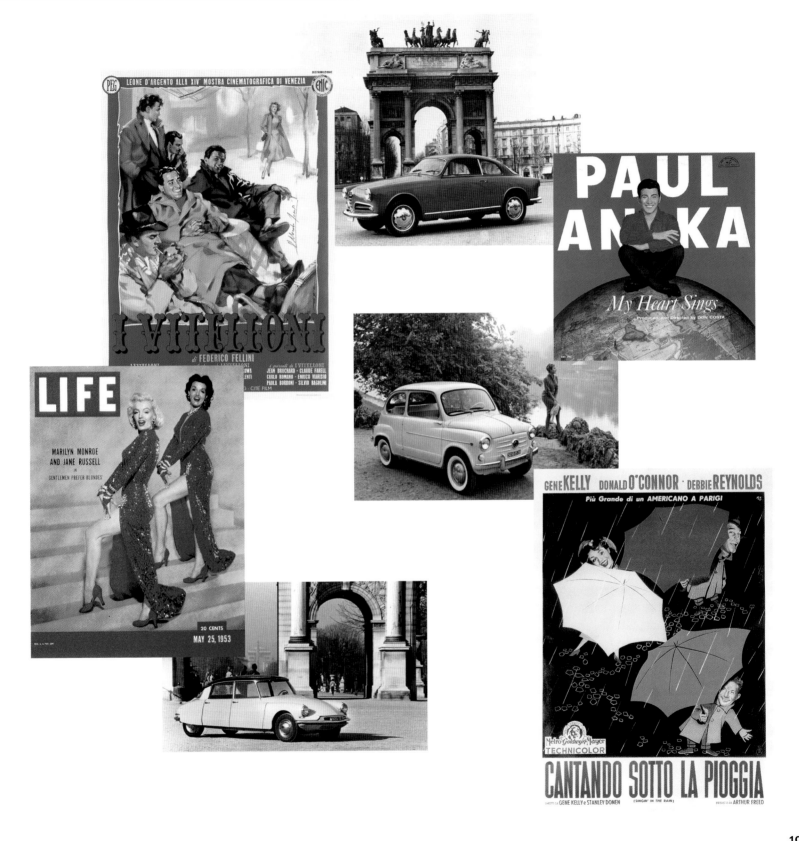

The '50s

... le belle domeniche in *Vespa*

La Vespa ha trasformato la nostra vita!

VESPA 125 L. 128.000	Oggi non siamo più fra quelli che guardano malinconicamente gli altri che partono.
VESPA 150 L. 148.000	Oggi, grazie alla Vespa, siamo fra quelli che partono, fra quelli che vanno a divertirsi.
VESPA 150 G.S. L. 178.000	La settimana trascorre rapida e lieto nel pensiero della domenica.
Condizioni rateali a 12-16-20-24 mesi	La nostra Vespa è sicura, confortevole, elegante ed economica.... son due ruote che ne valgono quattro.

E anche un mezzo ideale per il lavoro!

LA PIÙ GRANDE PRODUZIONE MONDIALE DI SCOOTERS

By the Fifties the Vespa was already an enormously successful product. The first calendars appeared, the scooter was seen on the covers of magazines and on film posters. The Vespa became recreational transport not solely a means of reaching work. The success was such as to generate the models built under license in various countries: Great Britain, France, Germany, Spain, Belgium. As the Vespa became more widespread, the first clubs were formed and owners had the opportunity to participate in numerous rallies.

There were two displacements, 125 (base and U) and 150 cc (base and GS). The transmission now used flexible cables rather than the rigid rods. Two particularly sporty models were also introduced, the Sport and the Sei Giorni, both produced in limited numbers. The general public was, however, won over by the GS 150 that boasted a number of innovations: it was the first Vespa fitted with 10" wheels and a four-speed gearbox.

In 1956, Piaggio was the world's largest motorcycle manufacturer with an output of 221 thousand units. That same year, Pontedera celebrated the production of the millionth Vespa.

While marketing had yet to be become a buzzword in Italy, Piaggio had come up with a perfect sales formula. In those years, the company had put together a winning combination of hire purchase, a one-year guaran-

The Piaggio workforce crowd around the 500,000th Vespa built to celebrate the event (29 October 1953).

The '50s

The '50s

tee, free maintenance coupons and a free theft and third-party insurance policy: how could one resist? Then, in 1954, came a masterstroke when the price of the 125 was dropped from 150,000 to 128,000 lire.

Post-war reconstruction had now been completed and Italy was enjoying a period of growth that was to be defined as the "boom" and the "economic miracle". Italian homes began to be equipped with domestic appliances as the first refrigerators and washing machines appeared. Television was born and these were the years of the famous quiz show *Lascia o raddoppia* (similar to *The $ 64,000 Question*), with the bars crammed with people determined not to miss a single episode. Even the cinemas were forced to cancel screenings on the evenings when the quiz show was broadcast. Within this context the Vespa became increasingly popular and could be seen in any urban location shots in the films of the period – when it was not actually playing a starring role as in *Roman Holiday*. Midway through the decade, a cyclone blew through the world of personal transport: Fiat presented its 600, the first utility car accessible to the masses. It was above all the two-wheeled sector that felt the effects with a vertical fall in sales as many clients, perhaps making recourse to delayed payments, finally moved up to four wheels. However, the Vespa had a different clientele and it was actually in this period that it consolidated its success.

The '50s

The Millionth Vespa

PONTEDERA - 28 APRILE 1956

There were great festivities on the 28th of April 1956, with Piaggio celebrating not only the first 10 years of the Vespa, but also the millionth example to leave the Pontedera production lines. In order to mark the event Piaggio invited Italian and foreign authorities, hundreds of journalists from throughout the world and dozens of agents from Italy and abroad. When the millionth Vespa rolled off the line it was actually blessed by the Archbishop of Florence. Piaggio printed a celebratory envelope seal and the Italian Post Office granted a special frank for all correspondence leaving the internal Pontedera factory office.

The event was truly remarkable if you think that the production of the 500,000th Vespa had been celebrated on the 29th of October 1953. It had taken seven years to reach the first half million and just two and a half for the second. This gives some idea of the success and the boom in sales recorded by the Vespa in the early Fifties when it accounted for 34% of the entire motorcycle and scooter market.

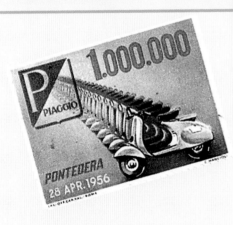

The '50s

From *Motociclismo*, 9th of March 1950:

Four years have now passed since the Vespa made its first, almost timid public appearance early in the spring of 1946. The Vespa immediately appealed to everyone without hesitation, in spite of its appearance that most felt to be decidedly revolutionary. This machine with its new and attractive line, with its completely enclosed engine, with its open frame allowing the rider to sit on the saddle without having to straddle the rear wheel, with no pretensions to speed, quiet and designed to protect the clothes of the rider, immediately won over all those who felt the need for a means of personal transport but would never have had the courage to use a true motorcycle. And it is by no means a common occurrence that Piaggio, despite being totally new to the construction of motor vehicles, managed to identify to perfection the tastes and requirements of the practically virgin clientele to which it turned and to *create for it a vehicle that from the very first example has proved to be so well thought out as to require subsequently no substantial modifications. The only changes of note were the increase the engine's displacement from 98 to 125 cc and the adoption of a more efficient sprung suspension system, both being introduced at the request of the clientele, who having taken to the new scooter, wanted to use it for even the most demanding of duties and therefore required far greater performance than originally planned for.*

This interesting testimony underlines how the arrival of the Vespa constituted a "revolutionary" episode in the two-wheeled world, bringing the new scooter to a clientele "that would never have had the courage" to tackle a conventional motorcycle for the first time.

The rapid spread of the Vespa in the 1950s was in part due to the extraordinary promotional activities of the numerous Vespa Clubs in Italy and abroad.

The '50s

— Buon giorno, nonno!
— Bonjour grand'père!
— Hi there Grand pop!
(Motocycles - Paris)

* * *

* * *

Dittatura stradale.
Prepotence routiere.
Road hog.
(Candido - Milano)

... meglio una Vespa oggi
che un automobile domani ...

Part two

THE ROAD TO SUCCESS

The '60s

The '6os

CINEMA
007 James Bond (Robert Young) - *La Dolce Vita* (Federico Fellini) - *Il Sorpasso* (Dino Risi) - *The Magnificent Seven* (John Sturges) - *The Graduate* (Mike Nichols)

MUSIC
Love Me Do (Beatles) - *Blowing in the Wind* (Bob Dylan) - *Satisfaction* (Rolling Stones) - *Ventiquattromila baci* (Adriano Celentano)

TV
Civilisation - Arcobaleno - Dr Who - Z Cars - Star Trek - The Odyssey - The Citadel

BOOKS
Tropic of Cancer (Henry Miller) - *Farewell to Arms* (Ernest Hemingway) - *One Hundred Years of Solitude* (Gabriel Garcìa Màrquez)

CARS
Mini - Ferrari 250 GTO - Alfa Romeo Giulia - Lancia Fulvia - Jaguar E-Type - Porsche 911

MOTORCYCLES
Aermacchi 250 Chimera - Ducati 200 Elite - Laverda 200 - Moto Guzzi 125 Stornello - BSA 650 A 65

FASHION
First collections by: Valentino (1960) - Kenzo (1961) - Cacharel (1962) - Benetton brothers go into business (1965) - Hippies

INNOVATIONS
Credit cards - Jet airliners - Photocopiers - Laser - Birth control pill - First heart transplant

ENTERTAINMENT
The Twist - Barbie - Super 8 - Peanuts - American Pop Art - Radio transmission "Chiamate Roma 3131" - Panini stickers

SPORT
Olympics: Rome, Tokyo and Mexico City - Eddy Merckx wins Giro d'Italia (1968) - Ferrari win Constructors' Championship (1961 and 1964)

EVENTS
Assassination of John F. Kennedy (1963) - Vajont landslide (1963) - Florence flooding (1966) - Neil Armstrong first man on the moon (1969)

GARCÍA
MÁRQUEZ

CENT'ANNI
DI SOLITUDINE

PUNTₑMES
APERITIVO
un punto di amaro e mezzo di dolce

The '60s

Towards the mid–sixties, there was a sudden decline in sales in Italy. Everyone now wanted a car, even the most basic model, and the scooter market suffered. In 1965 Piaggio recorded an operating loss of over 300 million lire, a figure that rose to a billion in 1966. Damage to the company was limited by the success enjoyed by a new model, the Vespa 50. Born in 1963, the model enjoyed immediate success thanks to the fact that it was exempt from the obligatory registration number and driving licence required by the Italian Highway code for vehicles of above 50 cc. The advertising campaign was therefore aimed at young people (the 50 could be ridden at 14), a new target group that from then on was to be an increasingly important component of the Vespa clientele. Student numbers were increasing and the Vespa 50 was the ideal vehicle to take them to school. Thanks to its compact dimensions and reduced weight, the Vespa 50 appealed to women as well as satisfying youthful desires for emancipation, freedom and independence. Piaggio also introduced the Elestart version with standard electric starting. In order to attract even more fourteen-year-olds, the company presented a moped at the Genoa Fair of the Sea on the 11th of October 1967 that was to symbolize an era. Numerous models were introduced during the 1960s as along-

la Piaggio presenta il nuovo modello

1961

Vespa 150

- motore migliorato – maggiore elasticità e ripresa
- carburatore con dispositivo per avviamento immediato
- impianto elettrico con elevate caratteristiche fotometriche

cambio a 4 velocità

PREZZO **L. 148.000**
VENDITE RATEALI A 6-12-16-20-24 MESI

lo scooter più venduto nel mondo

The '60s

con vespa **si può**

side the 50 were the 90 models (base and SS), the small-frame 125 (Nuova), large-frame 125 (base, Super and GT), the 150 (base, GL, Super and Sprint), 160 (GS) and 180 (SS and Rally).

In the early Sixties, all riders of two-wheeled vehicles were faced with an unaccustomed bureaucratic obstacle: the obligatory driving licence. Would Piaggio abandon its Vespisti in their hour of need? No, of course not. The firm organized courses at Vespa Club d'Italia premises to help its clients pass the test.

A great flood devastated the Pontedera district on the 4th of November 1966 when the River Era broke its banks and inundated the Pontedera factory. Thanks to the efforts of the workforce, the furnaces were shut down before the rising waters could cause an explosion.

During this decade there were further significant Vespa sales milestones. The two millionth example was celebrated in the July of 1960 and the three millionth in the March of 1965, while the four millionth came off the production line in the May of 1969. Progress was therefore constant, a million units being sold every five years despite the difficulties of the market. 1964 saw the completion of the Autostrada del Sole from Milan to Naples.

in tutto il mondo

The '60s

The hexagonal Piaggio logo

Piaggio changed its logo on the 1st of October 1967. The new version was a blue hexagon with an arrow symbol. This symbol may also be seen as a mirror image double "P". With this change the company wanted to underline the major corporate revision undertaken in that period. The aeronautical and railway business was separated from the motor vehicle division, the company was reconfigured and the managerial structure was modified. The new chairman was Umberto Agnelli, the son-in-law of Enrico Piaggio.

The introduction of the new logo was announced to the press, the Italian dealers and the foreign importers and an entire issue of the *Piaggio Magazine* was devoted to of the changes: «This introduction will be, where possible, immediate and total, involving both vehicles and advertising; in other sectors, where this is not possible, it will be more gradual.» The period in which the old and new logos co-existed, brief as it was, has to be considered as a sensitive moment with regard to the image of the brand with respect to the consumers. The extreme importance of this

delicate operation and the need for the complete cooperation did not escape the Italian dealers and the foreign importers».

Naturally, such a significant change was reflected throughout the organization, from the office signing and that of the dealerships, from advertising to letterheads. It is interesting to note how this logo remained unchanged for 35 years of Vespa production. Following the error committed in the 1990s when the very name Vespa was rejected in favour of Cosa, in the new millennium the firm recognised that it was a key element in the valorization of the product.

From this point of view, everything possible was done to revive historical references, introducing diverse elements that were recognisable from previous models. This has led to the reappearance of the original shield, the one with the diagonal division and light and dark blue colouring. A smart decision, and one well received by many enthusiasts who, while being tied to the image of the hexagon, could hardly remain indifferent to a symbol so laden with history.

Stabilimenti Piaggio di Pontedera: una linea di montaggio Vespa.

5.300 punti di assistenza contraddistinti da insegne col marchio Piaggio Servizio sono distribuiti su tutto il territorio nazionale. Le parti di ricambio utilizzate sono le stesse che vengono prodotte negli impianti di Pontedera e montate sui veicoli nuovi di fabbrica.

con Vespa si può

The '60s

...per mettere in moto la Vespa 50 è sufficiente un colpo di pedivella...

15

...il suo uso non richiede abbigliamenti speciali, nè tute, stivali, giacconi od altro...

29

Part two

THE ROAD TO SUCCESS

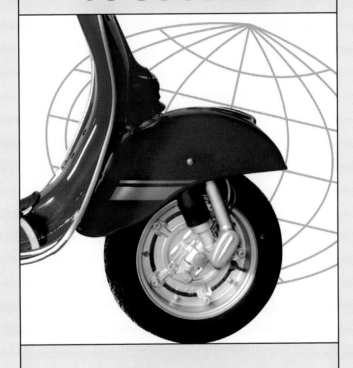

The '70s

The '70s

CINEMA
Love Story (George Hiller) - *Saturday Night Fever* (John Badham) - *Il Padrino* (F. F. Coppola) - *Star Wars* (George Lucas) - *Amarcord* (Federico Fellini)

MUSIC
Let it be (Beatles) - *Wild World* (Cat Stevens) - *The Dark Side of the Moon* (Pink Floyd) - *Daniel* (Elton John) - *Staying Alive* (Bee Gees)

TV
First colour transmissions in Italy (1975) - HBO via cable - Charlie's Angels - Rischiatutto - Happy Days

BOOKS
The Invisible Cities (Italo Calvino) - *La Storia* (Elsa Morante) - *The Interior Life* (Alberto Moravia) - *A Man* (Oriana Fallaci)

CARS
Fiat 126/127 - Ford Fiesta - BMW 3 and 5 series - Range Rover - Ferrari Daytona/BB - Lamborghini Countach - Lancia Stratos

MOTORCYCLES
Honda 750 - Kawasaki 500 - Suzuki 750 - Moto Guzzi V7 750 - Laverda SF 750 - Ducati Supersport 750 - Bimota KB1 - Mondial Touring 125

FASHION
Miniskirt - Hot pants - Tanga - Bell-bottoms Jeans- Big collars - Wigs and toupees - Ray Ban sunglasses - Man's handbag

INNOVATIONS
Boeing 747 Jumbo - Fibre optics - Pocket calculator - First Apple personal computer - Colour television - VHS video recorders

ENTERTAINMENT
Videogames - Bic lighters - Kinder eggs - Post-Its - Pulsar watch - Discos - Clik Claks - Action Man

SPORT
Olympics: Munich and Montréal - Thöni wins three skiing World Cups - Munari World Rally Champion - Ferrari win Constructors' Championship

EVENTS
Divorce and abortion legalised - World oil crisis - End of the Vietnam war - Watergate - Beatles break up - Birth of rap music

The '70s

This was a decade of light and shadow. Following the crisis of the 1960s, attempts were made at Pontedera to invest significant resources in the youth market. In this period the dreams of countless fourteen-year-olds were focussed on mopeds and Piaggio managed to satisfy this demand with a remarkably varied range of products. There was of course the Vespa 50, but it was not alone. In the years of the moped boom, the new Ciao enjoyed an exceptional degree of success and capillary distribution that was reinforced in 1973 with the introduction of the Bravo. Piaggio's acquisition of Gilera then allowed the firm to experiment with a scooter with innovative styling, the Eco, which flanked rather than replaced the Vespa. These were difficult years, with the decade witnessing no less than two energy crises. The first, in 1973, saw the price of petrol rapidly triple with the entire automotive sector thrown into disarray. Having a range of successful mopeds ensured Piaggio's survival. Nonetheless, the firm was looking to the future and continued to diversify its production activities. These were the years in which the firm acquired the Argom company (rubber goods) and Bendix (brake servos) and Borg Warner (limited-slip differentials) production licenses. Piaggio also produced a small agricultural tractor powered

Piaggio and Gilera

On the 26th of November 1969, at the Circolo della Stampa in Milan, Piaggio's managing director, Nello Vallecchi, publicly announced the acquisition of Gilera of Arcore.
From the *Piaggio* magazine of April 1970: «Today, with the support of the Piaggio marque, Gilera represents one of the strongest Italian companies in its sector, with a range of models capable of satisfying the demands of enthusiasts of all forms of motorcycling: from gentle touring to extreme off-road and trials».
From the very outset, Gilera's output had been characterised by interesting technical innovations that soon earned the firm a reputation around the world. The marque enjoyed significant sporting success, especially with its four-cylinder engines in the '30s and '40s. The Arcore-based company survived and was successfully revived thanks to the Piaggio buy-out.

The '70s

by the engine from the Ape MP. The second energy crisis in 1979 was tackled with a renewed policy of expansion. In the 1970s, the scooter was an extremely successful vehicle, flanking the motorcycle market and achieving significant results. The Vespa enjoyed a reputation for being a product that kept pace with the times although in this period it did lose some of the appeal it had enjoyed in previous decades: it no longer represented a novelty while the new superbikes, the dream of countless young men, began to make their appearance. While through to 1970 the motorcycle was largely a vehicle for those who could not afford a car, when the Honda 750 was presented large displacement bikes began to be objects of desire and were actually purchased as status symbols. Nonetheless, the Vespa success story continued apace: five years to reach the 5,000,000th example (September 1974) then just three years to reach the 6,000,000th (August 1977) and a further four to reach 7,000,000 (March 1981).

This represented an important achievement in a decade marked by the fuel crises of 1973 and 1979 that had serious consequences for the mobility and economies of all western countries. In Italy, the first car-free Sundays were introduced and the price of petrol rocketed.

The '70s

Per te che conosci la gioia della guida veloce. Per te che sai che un sorpasso è sicuro solo quando è sempre pronta una grande riserva di potenza. Per te che nello spunto da fermo, o nelle punte di velocità massima non vuoi essere secondo a nessuno. Per te abbiamo creato la Vespa Sprint Veloce.

The '70s

Part two

THE ROAD TO SUCCESS

The '80s

The '80s

CINEMA

Apocalypse Now (Francis F. Coppola) - *The Last Emperor* (Bernardo Bertolucci) - *E.T. and Indiana Jones* (Steven Spielberg) - *Blade Runner* (Ridley Scott)

MUSIC

Thriller (Michael Jackson) - *Every breath you take* (Police) - *Born in the USA* (Bruce Springsteen) - *Material Girl* (Madonna) - *Solo noi* (Toto Cotugno)

TV

Birth of CNN (June 1980), Canale 5, Rete 4 and Italia 1. Mixer - *Dallas* - Quelli della Notte - *Fame* - *Miami Vice*

BOOKS

The Name of the Rose and *Foucoult's Pendulum* (Umberto Eco) - *Satanic Verses* (Salman Rushdie) - *Palomar* (Italo Calvino) - *The Alchemist* (Paulo Coelho)

CARS

Renault Espace - Audi Quattro - Fiat Panda and Uno - Lancia Delta - Ferrari Testarossa - Mercedes Benz SEC

MOTORCYCLES

BMW R 80/GS - Ducati Paso 750 - Kawasaki GPZ 900 - Honda VFR 750 - Suzuki GSXR 750

FASHION

Milan capital of Italian fashion - Explosion of prêt-à-porter - Swatch watches - Timberland boat shoes - Moncler ski jackets - Nike and Reebok trainers

INNOVATIONS

Birth of the TGV high-speed train (1981) - ATMs - Portable video cameras - First Philips compact disc - Fax - First artificial heart - Apple Macintosh

ENTERTAINMENT

Cordless phones - Walkmar - Rubik's Cube - the Lambada - Teletext - Aerobics - Hot Wheels cars - Atari consoles

SPORT

Italy wins World Cup in Spain (1982) - Olympics: Moscow, Los Angeles and Seoul - Ferrari wins World Constructors' Championship (1982 and 1983)

EVENTS

Itavia DC9 crash at Ustica - Perestroika - Fall of the Berlin wall - Chernobyl disaster - Space Shuttle disintegrates on take-off

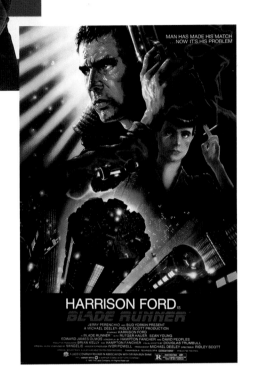

131

The '80s

Piaggio continued to pursue its policy of expansion and began producing automotive components in the Atessa factory. In 1981, Piaggio acquired the historic Bianchi firm, a producer of celebrated bicycles. In that same year, the company achieved its production record with an output of no less than 512,630 units, with a turnover of 626 billion lire in the process. The workforce also reached its highest ever total of 13,470 employees. However, the rest of the decade represented something of a decline. By 1989, for example, the total number of employees had dropped to 6000 reflecting a fall in demand for two-wheeled vehicles during the 1980s. The decline in sales was exacerbated by the introduction of new laws that obliged riders to wear helmets from 1986. Compared with 10 years earlier, the second half of the decade saw a veritable collapse with sales falling by 50%. The scooter market was suffering something of an image crisis and was hardest hit. Young people no longer saw this type of vehicle as a symbol of freedom and independence and scooter registrations in Italy precipitated. From the over 100,000 units of the early '80s the figure dropped to just 10,890 in 1990, with the market essentially being identified with the Vespa given that it had virtually no rivals.

The PK "seed"

From the PK brochure:

"Every Vespa is composed of 1400 pieces that during the course of 35 years of technical and stylistic evolution have been subjected to around 19,000 modifications. Today, thanks to this continuous evolution, only a single detail remains identical to the specification of the original design. A component the size of a seed around which everything has changed, but which to signifies the very seed of a success that is being renewed. This component, which we will never replace, is at the heart of our Vespa.

For the record, the "seed" in question is the flywheel magneto spline. The Vespa changes, but always remains the same. Such is the destiny of a unique industrial product. When the PK series was presented it was by no means difficult to recognise the mechanical and stylistic elements that identified it as a classic Vespa: the small diameter wheels, the steel monocoque, the two-stroke engine, the air cooling and the gripshift gear change. And yet... and yet the PK was an all-new Vespa, as it would

only logical to expect given that no less than 35 years had passed since the birth of the first model. This demonstrates that over the years, while the basic design remained unaltered, there has been a continuous process of evolution. Certainly, from the outside, at least for the non-Vespisti, it is sometimes hard to see the differences, with many models appearing virtually identical. From this point of view, the designers have always faced a major challenge: that of allowing the Vespa to evolve continuously through focussed interventions and small steps, without ever making perilous leaps forward. Piaggio cleverly emphasised with the "seed" campaign just how far the development of the Vespa has actually progressed. Practically nothing has remained interchangeable with the models of the past, all the components have gradually been improved and perfected. However, it would be nice to think that it was a gesture of affectionate recognition; it is nice to know that at least one piece, as small as it may be, has remained unchanged. And knowing how the Vespa story proceeded, it might be said that the "seed" has borne excellent fruit.

The '80s

The Vespa Nuova Linea was presented as follows in the PK catalogue: «Born as the present, born as the future. The present is born as a technical synthesis of the cardinal points of the Vespa. The present is born as the mature evolution of an ever-current technological concept. The future is born as the projection of a new aesthetic creed. The future is born to conjugate in time true values of safety and reliability. The Vespa Nuova Linea: a new dawn for the Vespa. The birth of the Piaggio programme for the '80s, a present-future programme».

These were difficult years. The general public was turning its back on motorcycles throwing the sector into crisis and even the scooter firms were also sailing through troubled waters. However, the period also saw the rise of many forms of alternative entertainment that involved young people in other sectors such as those of computers, charter flights, various forms of personal stereo and CDs. New trends appeared, the first Swatch watches went on sale, the first McDonald's opened in Italy and the first Italian private TV networks were developed. In this period Piaggio did all it could to remain competitive by renewing the two Vespa series, but the operation was only partially successful: the new large frame Vespa PX was as popular as the small frame PK was ignored.

Panasonic

Portable VHS Video System

NV-100 Video Cassette Recorder
WVP-50 Colour Video Camera

Part two

THE ROAD TO SUCCESS

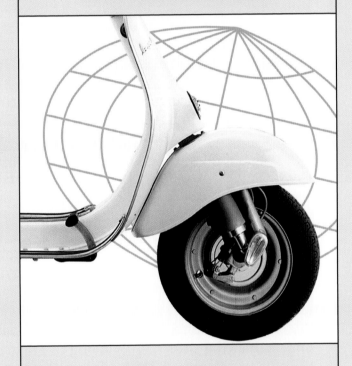

The '90s

The '90s

CINEMA

Life is Beautiful (Roberto Benigni) - *Pretty Woman* (Garry Marshall) - *Thelma & Louise* (Ridley Scott), *Braveheart* (Mel Gibson) - *Titanic* (James Cameron)

MUSIC

Graffiti (Prince) - *Dangerous* (Michael Jackson) - *Faithful* (Cranberries) - *Barbie Girl* (Aqua) - *Achtung Baby, Zooropa* (U2) - *Portami a ballare* (Luca Barbarossa)

TV

Birth of TG5 - Fantastico - La Ruota della Fortuna - Mille lire al mese - Il fatto - Carramba che sorpresa - Non è la RAI - La Piovra - *ER*

BOOKS

Sostiene Pereira (Antonio Tabucchi) - *The Celestine Prophecy* (James Redfield) - *The Pelican Brief* (John Grisham) - *Ocean Sea* (Alessandro Baricco)

CARS

Smart - Renault Twingo - Nissan Micra - Ford KA - Porsche Boxster - Dodge Viper - Daimler-Benz-Chrysler agreement - BMW buys Rolls Royce

MOTORCYCLES

Ducati 916 - Ducati Monster - Honda 900 Fireblade - Triumph Speed Triple 900 - Suzuki 1300 Hayabusa

FASHION

'60s and '70s revival (miniskirts, flared trousers, hippy dresses, wedges and punk clothes) - "Eco-ethnic-grunge" fashion

INNOVATIONS

Internet - Cell phones - Video cameras and palmtop computers - Apple iMac - Dolly the sheep: first cloning of a mammal - Viagra, the "blue pill"

ENTERTAINMENT

Rollerblades - Snowboard - Jacuzzis - Game Boy - Play Station - Introduction of GPS satellite navigation

SPORT

New Zealand wins the America's Cup - Tomba wins the skiing world cup - Ferrari wins F1 World Constructors title (1999)

EVENTS

Unification of Germany (1990) - "Tangentopoli" (1992) - Channel Tunnel (1994) - Birth of the European Union (1993)

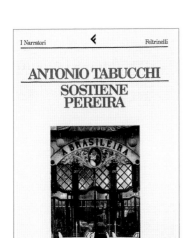

The '90s

Piaggio continued with its strategy of expansion and diversification with further acquisitions. In line with what was happening elsewhere in this period, attempts were made to diversify production as much as possible and Pontedera moved away from its historical roots and into the financial markets. The decade also saw a new chairman installed at Piaggio. In 1988, after 23 years in the job, Umberto Agnelli handed over the company reins to Gustavo Denegri. The organisational structure became more functional and a holding company was formed to head the group. From the 1st of January 1989 the general management moved from the historical offices in Genoa to Pontedera. Attempts were also made to profoundly renew the product lines in this decade. New scooter models were introduced for the first time as Piaggio tried to expand the market in the face of more incisive competition. The first of these new models was the Sfera featuring automatic transmission and plastic bodywork. It was followed by the Quartz, Zip and Skipper models that all enjoyed considerable sales success.

Cosa, what's in a name (extract from: *Cosa scooter project, the new generation*, Piaggio brochure, November 1987):
Piaggio is presenting a new scooter: the "Cosa". This is an avant-garde product in terms of aesthetic and technical contents, the

PX Classic: the last true Vespa?

The Classic version of the PX, launched in 1996, celebrated the 50th anniversary of the Vespa. Like all the models that had preceded it, the Classic featured a steel body with removable side-panels, a two-stroke engine, a gripshift gear change and drum brakes. If we also take into account the 10" wheels, the four-speed gearbox and the 2% oil/fuel mixture, we can see that the basic configuration was unchanged with respect to the GL introduced no less than 35 years earlier. However, moving into the new millennium everything changed: to the new ET series characterised, among other innovations, by a four-stroke engine and an automatic gearbox. And the PX? It still retained the monocoque with removable side-panels, the two-stroke engine and the gripshift. A front disc brake was adopted however, in place of the original drum. The PX thus enjoyed a new lease of life in Classic form as what many Vespisti have defined as the last "true" Vespa.

The '90s

levels of quality and reliability it offers and its comfort, roadholding and performance. Rather than an evolution of other products, the "Cosa" represents an innovative approach to design and technological applications and solutions to the problems of the scooter. The new scooter has a sleek, aggressive appearance. The styling, developed in the wind tunnel, is soft and aerodynamic. The ergonomic problems have been tackled and resolved with particular care in order to offer elevated comfort: the riding position, instrumentation and controls guarantee convenience and safety. Piaggio has invested 35 billion lire in the research and development project and the renewal of tooling.

It is never easy to find a name for a product with an international background and destination. Above all when this product is born in a sector, such as that of the scooter, in which for years Piaggio has enjoyed leadership with a vehicle called "Vespa" that has become the stuff of two-wheeled legend. A name was needed that was simple and communicative, valid in every language and perfectly at home in the world of youth. A new name. Not one bound up with an albeit glorious past, a name that opened to the future and represented a change of direction, a

All collectors naturally gravitate towards the most significant historic models, those that are well known for having introduced particular technical or styling features. In general these models are eagerly sought-after by enthusiasts and attract high prices. It might be of interest to take a look at the relatively recent models that could be of interest to collectors in the future. From this point of view the Classic is in pole position and from the outset promised to be an "instant collectible", much in the same way as the last air-cooled Porsche 911. The fortunate owners of the PX Classic have plenty to celebrate: their Vespa is the most highly evolved and developed of the drum-brake PX series and is already sought-after by collectors. Clearly a Vespa worth taking care of!

The '90s

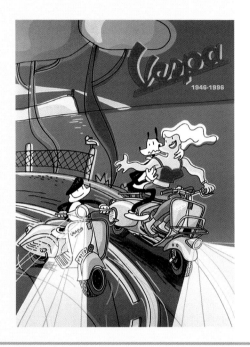

technical and industrial revolution expressed through a totally innovative scooter. Here, therefore, on the basis of careful studies and analyses, is the "Cosa". A courageous choice, but one that finds support in significant predecessors in the automotive and design fields. This is the case with the Fiat Uno and the Tizio, the world's most famous lamp. "Cosa", therefore, as the name/symbol of a new product. "Cosa" is easy, immediate, creative. A name suitable for a scooter that exalts Piaggio's technical experience and offers new horizons and opportunities for those that will use it. Quality and technology for lovers of two-wheeled transport. In the avant-garde with Piaggio.

These were difficult years for the Vespa: the large frame series was a commercial fiasco, not so much because it was unattractive but above all because it was called the Cosa, the small frame series did slightly better than in the previous decade, but was hardly a runaway success. Fortunately, the 50th anniversary of the Vespa in 1996 was exploited to launch in advance what was to be the Vespa of the third millennium. By the end of the decade things were looking far rosier and Piaggio was able to look confidently to the future.

The Vespa
at the Guggenheim

In 1998, a particularly important exhibition devoted to the motorcycle was inaugurated in New York. It was housed in the celebrated Guggenheim Museum, in the spiral building designed by Frank Lloyd Wright and located on the city's glamorous Fifth Avenue.

The title of the exhibition was "The Art of the Motorcycle" and there were not a few people who were surprised to see the world's most famous paintings replaced by motorcycles. However, the show was so successful that the organisers were obliged to extend its stay. It went on to become the most popular exhibition in the Guggenheim's history. Enthusiasts were able to admire the 100 most significant motorcycles of the 20th century including many examples of extraordinary historical value. Could the Vespa be left out? No, of course not. A fine 150 GS was in fact on display. It was just a shame about the colour: that yellow was never offered!

Part two

THE ROAD TO SUCCESS

The 2000s

The 2000s

CINEMA

The Lord of the Rings (Peter Jackson) - *Matrix* (The Wachowski Brothers) - *Mission Impossible* (Brian De Palma) - *Kill Bill* (Quentin Tarantino)

MUSIC

Come Away (Norah Jones) - *X & Y* (Coldplay) - *Tracks* (Vasco Rossi) - *Home* (Simply Red) - *Messaggio d'amore* (Matia Bazar) - *Per dire di no* (Alexia)

TV

Big Brother- Mai dire gol - *C.S.I.* - *Alias* - *Sex and the City* - *Desperate Housewives* - *Il Commissario Cordier* - *O.C.*

BOOKS

Harry Potter (J.K. Rowling) - *The Da Vinci Code* (Dan Brown) - *La pazienza del ragno* (Andrea Camilleri) - *Timeline* (Stephen King)

CARS

Enzo Ferrari - Toyota Prius - Alfa Romeo 159 - Renault Avantime - Lancia Thesis - BMW 1 - Hummer 3

MOTORCYCLES

MV Agusta F4 - Benelli Tornado - Aprilia RSV - Ducati 999 - Yamaha R1 - BMW R 1200 S - Suzuki GSR-600

FASHION

Return of: the little black dress, Dungarees, women's braces, the schoolgirl look, hot pants, pointed shoes, low waists - Guru t-shirts

INNOVATIONS

First photos of Titan by the European Huygens probe - Cloning of stem cells - First face transplant

ENTERTAINMENT

MP3 files - Apple iPod - Digital cameras - Videophones - Plasma TV screens

SPORT

Sydney, Athens and Peking Olympics, Turin Winter Olympics (2006) - Ferrari win World Constructors' Championship (2000, 2001, 2002, 2003, 2004)

EVENTS

New York 2001 Twin Towers terrorist attack - War in Iraq - EU expanded to 25 countries - Adoption of the Euro (2002)

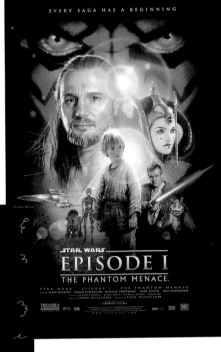

The 2000s

The Vespa approached the third millennium in fine form. The ever more chaotic urban traffic situation encouraged many motorists to forget their cars in favour of a vehicle better suited to wriggling through the jams and easier to park. This was a clientele that was not necessarily attracted to motorcycles and was actually looking for something that would offer greater protection and be closer to a car. In this period, the range of scooters available expanded greatly and many manufacturers offered interesting models. However, the Vespa remained unique, which accounted for much of its appeal. Technically, it was extremely up-to-date: it had a four-stroke engine and automatic transmission, but these were features common to all scooters. What the Vespa had that was unique was its history, it was the only scooter to have been in production since 1946. It was the only one with such a pedigree. Thanks in part to Roberto Colaninno's IMMSI group, the Vespa even found the resources to explore new markets such as that of the United States. Here the Vespa enjoyed great success, its presence expanding year by year to the point where it represented a true phenomenon. The range of models offered is wide and well defined. The small frame LX series is particularly suitable for

The 2000s

urban use thanks to its compact dimensions and great manoeuvrability. The large frame Granturismo series allows even highway and motorway trips to be undertaken in complete safety and even long distance touring is possible. For the die-hard Vespisti there is still the glorious PX with its rear brake pedal on the platform and a gripshift, just like back in 1946.

Piaggio heads for the Stock Exchange. The board of directors had hinted as much in the December of 2005 and it was confirmed on the 10th of March 2006. On that date, the Piaggio Group applied for inclusion on the Italian Stock Exchange's Telematic Share Market. This was the first step taken by the group led by Roberto Colaninno towards the placing of a part of the company capital. The coordinators of the offer are: Banca Caboto, Deutsche Bank, Citigroup, Mediobanca and Lehman Brothers. Following quotation, IMMSI intends to increase its share in the group from 40 to 54%, thus bring increasing stability and reinforcing the majority group.

The Vespa at the Fondazione Mazzotta

A major exhibition at the Fondazione Mazzotta's Milan headquarters was inaugurated in 2005. It featured the most important Italian motorcycles from a century of production history. They ranged from the Gilera of 1907 to the Grand Prix Ducati from 2004, with a large section being devoted to the Vespa. Pride of place was taken by the first model produced, the 98, naturally displayed lying on one side as at that time it had yet to be fitted with a stand. A rare racing Vespa and the streamlined record-breaker from 1951 could also be admired.

The 2000s

The Vespa-Ferrari, displayed in the Ferrari Store at Maranello, one of four examples of the ET4 150 created as a tribute to the Prancing Horse's Formula 1 triumph in 2000.

Part two

THE ROAD TO SUCCESS

The 2010s

The 2010s

CINEMA
Hugo Cabret (Martin Scorsese) - *Habemus Papam* (Nanni Moretti) - *La Grande Bellezza* (Paolo Sorrentino) - *The Social Network* (David Fincher)

MUSIC
Bad Romance (Lady Gaga) - *Till the World Ends* (Britney Spears) - *21* (Adele) - *Channel Orange* (Frank Ocean) - *Beyoncé* (Beyoncé)

TV
Il Commissario Montalbano - *Sex and the City* - *Dr House-Medical Division* - *Grey's Anatomy* - *South Park* - *House of Cards*

BOOKS
Fall of Giants (Ken Follett) - *Inferno* (Dan Brown) - *La Piramide di fango* (Andrea Camilleri) - *Fifty Shades of Grey* (E. L. James)

CARS
Tesla Model S - Alfa Romeo Giulietta - Ferrari F 12 Berlinetta - Lamborghini Aventador - Fiat 500 - Mini Countryman

MOTORCYCLES
Ducati Panigale - Ducati Scrambler - KTM Supeduke - Aprilia RSV4 - BMW RR - BMW GS - Kawasaki H2 - MA Agusta F3

FASHION
50's pin up style - gladiator sandals - ballet flats - Mirrored sunglasses -Low waist shorts - Low cost: Zara and H&M

INNOVATIONS
Robots in medicine - Smartwatch - Smartphone - Tablet - Curved screen TV - NASA: Mars Rover - 3D Printers

ENTERTAINMENT
iPhone - iPad - Kindle - Social Networks: Facebook, Twitter - Wikipedia - Over 10 MP cameras - Return of vinyl

SPORT
London (2012) and Rio de Janeiro (2016) Olympics. World Cup: won by Spain (2010) and Germany (2014)

EVENTS
Volcano in Iceland grounds European flights - Costa Crociere cruise liner wrecked off the Isola del Giglio - Steve Jobs dies - Expo 2015 in Milan

155

The 2010s

Piaggio came into this decade with well defined programmes: in-house, operating cost controls and monitoring procedures were reinforced and a major growth plan was implemented for the Research and Development areas. Externally, attention was devoted in particular to growth in Asia where the Vietnam factory was expanded and moves were made to establish another in India. A new research centre was also opened at Foshan in China.

At Pontedera, attention has instead focussed on the technological development of clean and economic internal combustion engines. Sectors that had previously been barely touched upon such as hybrid or electric propulsion units have been investigated. In order to keep the company tuned to ongoing changes, the Advanced Design Center was opened in Pasadena, California. A highly important event organized by Piaggio was the seminar "The Shape of Things to Come" held in 2015 in Milan in order to bring together the general public and leading world experts in technologies and the future.

The Vespa has always been at the centre of these initiatives and is increasingly becoming an independent brand. In this period the official Community was created: www.vespa.it/community, in order to help the ever greater number of Vespa enthusiasts to keep in touch.

The 2010s

1946 / 2010 - 70th Anniversary

Ahead of the great celebrations for the 70th anniversary in 2016, Piaggio presented a stunning array of novelties on its stand at Eicma in 2015. Cutting a fine figure were three models given dedicated colour schemes and new logos: the Primavera, GTS and PX. For each of these, the chosen livery is a delicate shade of blue, paired with a dark brown saddle. The side panels carry the "70°" logo referencing the anniversary, while a celebratory plaque is mounted on the back of the leg-shield. There are also dedicated accessories including a luggage rack and case. The fans were able to admire the new models alongside the legendary Vespa 98 that was brought in from the Pontedera museum for the occasion.

The 2010s

Part two

THE ROAD TO SUCCESS

The 2020s

The 2020s

The new decade opened in the midst of the dramatic Covid-19 pandemic, the consequences of which have affected every aspect of civil and industrial life. This meant that the celebrations for the 75th anniversary of the Vespa (2021) passed almost unnoticed and were effectively restricted to the production of a dedicated version. In reality there were two models, one for the small frame, with the Primavera (50, 125 and 150) and one for the large frame with the GTS 300. The models were distinguished by a metallic yellow livery and an eye-catching "75" logo on the side panels.

However, it was of course the Vespa Elettrica that brought the greatest innovations. The model was introduced in moped form (with a maximum speed of 45 kph), but this was soon replaced by the 125 version, with a maximum speed of 70 kph. This is the most innovative Vespa ever produced: the revolution that is encouraging manufacturers to replace the internal combustion engine with electric motors has swept through Pontedera and has brought with it a new generation of Vespas looking to the future.

The 2020s

The 2020s

The 2020s

Interview with Marco Lambri, head of the Piaggio Group's Styling Centre.

Q. When was the project born?

A. *We started working on it in 2014 and the first prototype was presented at the EICMA show in Milan in November 2016.*

Q. Was the Vespa your first choice, or were other scooters considered?

A. *From the outset the technology was conceived to be transversal, applicable to a series of vehicles, but the Vespa was chosen to introduce it to the market. This had already been the case with other technological innovations (ABS, LCD and the 3V engine) that were introduced on the Vespa and then extended to the rest of the scooter range.*

Q. Was it always the small frame or was the large frame also considered?

A. *We immediately turned to the small frame due to a question of energy balance.*

Q. Are there plans for the large frame in the future?

A. *The electric traction sector is expanding rapidly; it's hard to predict all the applications that might be developed.*

Q. What were the major problems that had to be overcome?

A. *The greatest challenge was that that of respecting the elegance and style of the Vespa, while introducing new technology. We also had to retain space under the saddle for a helmet and ensure that innovative "digital" elements such as the TFT instrumentation could coexist with the "analogue" components that are integral parts of the classic Vespa style.*

Q. And the choice of colours?

A. *We immediately settled on a single metal colour in order to underline the exclusiveness of the monocoque steel frame and to emphasise our respect for a unique tradition, even in the presence of such and important innovation. A single colour, but one embellished with diverse contrasting trim elements in bright colours, chosen by the client. Shield edging, saddle, wheels and other details, coordinated in a package that contrasted with the metallic paint of the frame.*

Q. An internal, non-removable battery.

A. *It is much more likely that a Vespa will be kept in a garage with a power supply, rather than being left in the street at night. For this first version, therefore, we went for the non-removable battery configuration (in part also due to the size of the batteries).* □

THE VESPA FAMILY

The Vespa abroad

Beyond the borders

Places to go! . . . things to do! . . . you're part of today's vibrant crowd that's on the go. So go with style . . . go with fun and excitement . . . go on a Sears Scooter. We'll show you three versatile beauties . . . all sleek 'n sassy, surging with power and lots of get-up-and-go to match your adventurous spirit.

The Vespa's success was not confined to Italy. The scooter also became an extremely popular vehicle elsewhere, with a huge following, especially in Europe. Many manufacturers attempted to compete with Pontedera on their local markets with models of all shapes and sizes, but without success. Whether those manufacturers were called BSA or Triumph (in England), Peugeot or Motobécane (in France), NSU or Zündapp (in Germany), not one managed to produce a scooter to rival the Italian model. In many countries, the Vespa itself thus began to be produced under license. ACMA was born in France, with its production lines in the Fourchambault turning out not only standard models but also a version for military use carrying a large cannon. A more traditional Vespa was built in Germany, first by Hoffman and then by Messerschmitt, and in England, by Douglas. Compared with the original models, the variations generally concerned just a few components, including the front headlight, which was changed to meet local regulations. The major exception was the Russian Viatka, a straight copy… and built without a license.

The Vespa abroad

Modell A

Ein wirklich volkstümliches Fahrzeug zu einem Preis, der für einen Motorroller, besonders jedoch für die VESPA, einmalig ist. Bewußt wurde an der Ausstattung gespart. Dennoch vermittelt auch dieses Modell die so typischen VESPA-Vorteile: Formschöne Linienführung, robuster Motor mit der bekannten hervorragenden Leistung und große Wirtschaftlichkeit, dazu die überlegene Straßenlage durch wirksame Federung mit zusätzlicher hydraulischer Dämpfung. Die VESPA A ist der Motorroller für den Berufsverkehr, er bleibt denjenigen vorbehalten, die in dem Motorroller ein solides Gebrauchsfahrzeug sehen.

France

ACMA

The Vespa was built under license by ACMA in its factory at Four-chambault. Two models were offered, the 125 and the 125 GL. In contrast with Pontedera's 150, the ACMA version was fitted with an engine derived from that of the 125 and had different bore and stroke dimensions.

However, the most interesting ACMA model was the military Vespa. The project was initiated in 1953 when the French army decided to replace its now obsolete American Cushman scooters that dated from the Second World War. A competition was organised with the Valmobile 100, the Bernardet 250 and the Vespa 150 being entered. The eventual winner was the Vespa and production got underway in 1956. Designated as the TAP 56 and revised in 1959 as the TAP 59 (TAP standing for Troupes Aéro Portées), the military Vespa was finished in a typical dark olive green only and was produced exclusively in France. It boasted a number of special features, including a reinforced frame as it was designed to be able to be parachuted. What is most striking, however, is the presence of a 3" cannon protruding from the leg-shield, while on either side the side-panels were fitted with ammunition racks. 500 examples of the military Vespa were constructed and the vehicle saw active service in Algeria and Indochina.

The Vespa abroad

Belgium

MISA

The Vespa models marketed in Belgium came out of the MISA factory at Jette, near Brussels. Production ran from 1954 to 1962 with 125 and 150 cc versions of the GS series being offered. The Belgian Vespa was initially distributed by Bevelux, with an organisation extending into Holland and Luxemburg. There were over 150 sales outlets, but Vespas could also be purchased at a number of major stores in Brussels including: Bon Marché, Galeries Anspach, Innovation, Grands magasins de la Bourse and Cado-Radio.

When the marketing side was handled directly by MISA the network was extended with over 400 dealerships being established in Belgium. The 125 was sold at 16,200 Belgian francs, with the 150 offered at 17,500 BF. The more expensive 150 GS was instead available for 19,900 BF.

Even the Ape series was offered: the first model to be distributed was Tipo C, on sale from 1957. In order to encourage sales, the Ape was offered with a 36-month instalment plan.

There was great interest in the Vespa on the local market and the production lines were kept running at full capacity: no less than 55 examples of the Vespa and the Ape left the factory each day in 1958.

Germany

Die *Vespa* mit dem *Vespa*-Seitenwagen

ist eine harmonische, vollendet aufeinander abgestimmte Konstruktion. Hier haben Sie das richtige Gefährt für eine Fahrt zu zweien! Man sitzt in dem geräumigen Seitenwagen äußerst bequem, angenehm gefedert und vor Fahrtwind geschützt.

Technische Daten:

Fahrgestell geschweißte Rohrkonstruktion, Anschluß durch Rohrtraverse. Weiche Federung, Windschutzscheibe, Getriebeübersetzungen der Beiwagenmaschine: 12,2:1, 8,2:1, 5,83:1 Eigengewicht des Gespannes 130 kg; zulässiges Gesamtgewicht des Gespannes 285 kg. Lackierung: Fischsilbergrau, Vespa-grün.

Hoffmann-Werke LINTORF BEZ. DÜSSELDORF

HOFFMANN/ MESSERSCHMITT

From 1950, the Vespa was built under license in Germany by Hoffmann of Lindorf, near Dusseldorf. After 1955, production was instead organised at the Messerschmitt works at Augsburg in Bavaria. Two models were offered, the 150 Touren and the 150 GS. It is interesting to note that Messerschmitt had a good reputation in the aeronautical industry, just like Piaggio. The Vespa was exported to Germany after 1956.

In Germany the Vespa failed to attract the same degree of success it enjoyed in other countries such as Great Britain and France. Among the various motives were those associated with the local Highway Code: the same driving licence and level of insurance was required whether a vehicle had a displacement of 100 cc or 250 cc. For this reason, there was no demand for the classic 125 cc displacement with the market preferring large displacement scooters with imposing dimensions. Of the 124,000 scooters sold in 1955, 32,000 were built by Zündapp (Bella), 27,000 by NSU (Prima), 16,000 by Heinkel (Tourist) with just 900 being Vespas. Messerschmitt therefore abandoned distribution in 1964 with Piaggio operating directly on the German market from the following year.

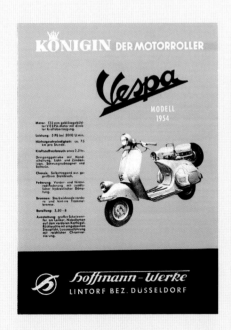

Great Britain

Douglas

Licensed production of the Vespa in Great Britain began in 1951 at the Douglas works in Kingswood, near Bristol. Two engine displacements were again offered, 125 and 150 cc with the last also available in GS form. Production ceased in 1957, with a total of 126,000 examples having been sold. While it was not as economical a machine as it was in Italy, the British Vespa enjoyed a degree of success and was widely used by the police forces. It also became an essential part of the Mod lifestyle, as seen in the cult film *Quadrophenia*. The sales strategy adopted in Britain saw the Vespa positioned as a high quality vehicle, with highly elegant and bowler-hatted aristocratic figures being photographed with their scooters (and even with their chauffeurs!).

In this period the Vespa became an extremely fashionable vehicle and numerous clubs were soon founded. In 1953 there were no less than 60 Vespa clubs with over 3000 members. In the July of that year a national rally was organised at Brighton with over 500 Vespisti taking part. Many important British trendsetters were also photographed on their Vespas: from the Duke of Edinburgh to the Formula 1 driver Stirling Moss.

Spain

Moto Vespa

From 1956, the Vespa was built under license in Spain by Moto Vespa at Ciudad Lineal, near Madrid. Output comprised the 50, 125 Super and 150 Sprint models.

The Moto Vespa factory occupied 21,000 m² where the complete production cycle took place. The launch of the various models was accompanied by an advertising campaign highlighting the vast range of potential clients: from the student to the hunter, from the priest to the doctor. There was also a comparison with the world of the automobile, the scooter as usual being presented as a "small two-wheeled car". In order to create images of great impact, events were organised in the arenas where toreadors would perform aboard Vespas. In Spain too the Vespisti congregated in clubs that grew year by year. The first president of the Vespa Club of Spain was Don Luis Serrano de Pablo who, together with his wife Dona Matilde, travelled to the Vatican to donate a chalice to Pope Pius XII.

In contrast with other European countries, production in Spain continued through the following decades.

The 125 Primavera of the 1970s was sold for 16,900 pesetas, the 125 PX from the 1980s for 280,000 pesetas and the Cosa from the 1990s for 360,000 pesetas.

USSR

Viatka

From 1957, the Viatka 150 was built at Kirov in central Russia, then part of the Soviet Union of course. It was to all intents and purposes a Vespa 150, but rather than being built under license, it was a straight copy. The Viatka was named after the river that flowed near the factory, a typical custom in the Soviet Union in that period. The differences with respect to the original Vespa were minor but numerous. In terms of the engine they ranged from the displacement (from 145 to 148 cc) to the compression ratio (from 6.3:1 to 6.7), from the carburettor (from 18 to 200 mm) to the clutch (from 3 to 4 plates). With regard to the rest of the vehicle, the most distinctive feature was the wheels fitted with wider tyres (4.00 rather than 3.50"). As the monocoque was built from thicker steel, the Viatka was around 10 kilos heavier. Given the impossibility of asserting its rights to industrial protection regarding the product, Piaggio made recourse to irony. In a publication from 1959 a title proclaimed "They Make Satellites but Copy Scooters". The first man-made satellite was, in fact, launched by the Soviet Union, with the Sputnik being sent into orbit in 1957.

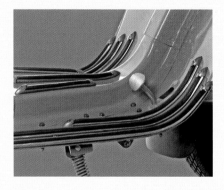

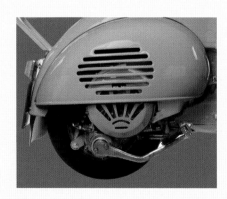

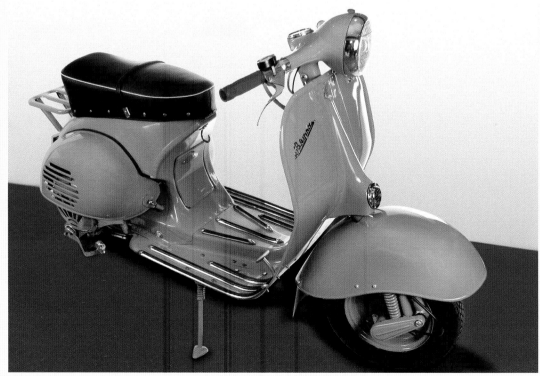

India

Bajaj

The Vespa was built under license in India by Bajaj from 1961, in the Poona factory near Bombay. It is still in production. The full name of the company is Bajaj Auto and it is in fact a large group whose main focus is on the production of cars; the scooter represents something of a sideline. The founder is proud to point out in his catalogues that he was a disciple of Mahatma Gandhi.

The Vespa was imported to India from as early as 1948. Bajaj then signed an agreement with Piaggio to build the various models locally before becoming independent in 1972. The first model to be manufactured at Poona was the Chetak, introduced in 1974. Production has continued into the third millennium with no significant technical or stylistic variations: the styling reflects that of the models built at Pontedera in the 1970s. The Indian models are all recognisable by the size of glovebox behind the leg-shield, much larger than those of the original models. The market is enormous and the Vespa-Bajaj is hugely popular in India. Over 4 million examples have been produced and in 2000 the vehicles circulating with the Bajaj marque numbered over 13millions. Remarkably, the Vespa-Bajaj has also been imported to Italy.

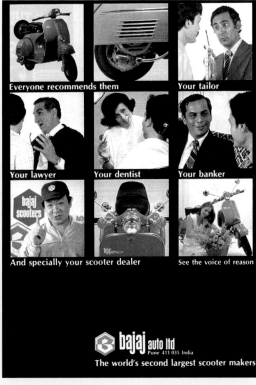

United States

Vespa of America

The 1970s saw the establishment in the USA of the Vespa of America Corporation. In this case scooters were not produced locally, but a number of models were imported: the 90 Sport, 125 Primavera, 150 Super and 200 Rally. In order meet US regulations a number of components were modified: indicators were added to the handlebars and side-panels, the rear light was detached from the body, the fuel tap was enlarged and reflectors were added to the side of the front mudguard. Sales ceased in 1981 but were revived in 2002. "Quick. What's the Vespa?" this was an advertising slogan used by the Vespa of America Corporation in the late '70s. In the United States there were still relatively few people with any awareness of the world's best-selling scooter. The American market is not easy and after just ten years Piaggio pulled the plug on its US operation. It was a hard decision to make, but understandable. In the USA, the public is accustomed to large vehicles such their V8 cars and Harley Davidson motorcycles; it is by no means easy to make inroads with a tiny scooter. Moreover, local laws are far stricter with regard to two-stroke engines that pollute more than four-stroke units.

Vespa 200 Rally. The largest Vespa is a lot more machine than you'd think. It's even legal on freeways. There's a locking storage compartment in front. Just like the most advanced automobiles, it has electronic assisted ignition.

Vespa 125 Primavera. Similar in size to the 90, but with a larger engine and 4-speed transmission. The Primavera will do 50 mph, so it's great for weekend jaunts as well as basic transportation in town.

Vespa 150 Super. The dressed-up 150 comes with a seat behind the driver's, and more chrome to dress it up. Smaller 8" wheels make it easy to maneuver in city traffic.

Vespa 90 Sport. Even the smallest Vespa comes with all you need for basic transportation. Carries two comfortably at speeds up to 40 mph.

La dolce Vespa.

The Vespa P200E.

Anyone who appreciates "the sweet life" will likewise appreciate La dolce Vespa, "the sweet Vespa Scooter."

Vespa Scooters have welded, unitized bodies for safety and comfort. The unique design lets you ride inside with your feet on the floor. And direct drive to the rear wheel means there's no chain to stretch or break.

You'll find a Vespa Scooter is clean, quiet, incredibly powerful and easy to handle. And you can expect between 70 and 140 mpg. So you'll save plenty of gas and money.

Today's Vespa Scooter is the result of 30 years of engineering refinement. Our top models offer sophistications like electronic ignition, automatic oil injection and exclusive damped hydraulic front suspension. With a hidden spare wheel included as

standard equipment. And the Vespa P200E, largest of three models, will take you anywhere. Even on the freeway.

Vespa products are made in Italy by Piaggio. Over the years, they've sold over 6,000,000 Scooters and 2,000,000 Mopeds. Which adds up to billions of dependable miles around the world. That's why both Vespa Scooters and Mopeds come with a 12-month warranty, with no limit on mileage.

Why not add La dolce Vespa to your life. You'll find your nearest Vespa dealer in the Yellow Pages. Or write to the address below.

Mileage is based on CUNA Standards. Yours may vary. Check Vespa limited warranty with your Vespa dealer. Wear helmet and eye protection. Check local laws. Vespa of America Corporation. Piaggio Group. 355 Valley Drive. Brisbane, CA 94005.

give your life a little vespa

WOW. WHAT WAS THAT?

Something very special is taking to the roads of America. A totally unique variety of two-wheel transportation: The Vespa scooter.

There have been more than 6 million Vespa scooters and 2 million Vespa mopeds sold around the world, with good reason.

The Vespa scooter's superior convenience and comfort has made it a valuable supplement to the automobile. You ride inside—clean and quiet—with your feet securely on the floor.

The low center of gravity increases control and maneuverability.

The engine, fuel tank and direct drive system are all below and behind you, in a welded, unitized body.

The top models offer freeway speed power plus electronic ignition, automatic oil injection, hydraulic front and rear suspension and a hidden spare tire.

Rather than being all engine and tires, the Vespa scooter is all beauty. Its exquisite Italian design is a remarkable

pairing of panache and practicality. Over 30 years of engineering excellence and experience guarantees it. It's all in a machine that wiggles in and out of traffic while delivering between 70 and 140 mpg. Plus a 12-month, unlimited mileage warranty.

For a test ride, see your Vespa dealer now. Look in the Yellow Pages or write us for nearest location. And next time your friends wonder what went by—it'll be you.

Mileage is based on CUNA Standards. Yours may vary. Check with your Vespa dealer. Wear helmet and eye protection. Check local laws. Vespa of America, 355 Valley Drive, Brisbane, CA 94005.

vespa
THE UNCOMMON CARRIER

QUICK. WHAT'S A VESPA?

Would you believe it's one of the world's most popular motor vehicles?

That's because it's also one of the world's most sensible, sophisticated street machines. The Vespa scooter. Not a motorcycle, not a motorbike, it's more like a two-wheeled car. You ride inside—cleanly and quietly —with your feet securely on the floor, protected by a welded, unitized body.

Its low center of gravity gives you a welcome sense of comfort, control and maneuverability.

Inside the top models lies an engine powerful enough for freeway driving and an automatic oil injection. There's electronic ignition and hydraulic front and rear suspension—even a hidden spare tire. Vespa scooters deliver between 70 and 140 mpg. Their stylish, sculptured body is delivered to you by super Italian designers.

We're talking about something Americans have seldom seen, yet are becoming increasingly interested in as a supplemental, sophisticated transportation. The Vespa scooter. It's the result

of over 30 years of engineering excellence and experience. More than 6 million Vespa scooters and 2 million Vespa mopeds have been produced and sold so far. No wonder it's backed by a 12-month, unlimited mileage warranty.

For a test ride, see your Vespa dealer now. Look in the Yellow Pages or write us for nearest location. The Vespa scooter is a totally unique riding experience. We invite you to experience it now at your local Vespa dealer's. Look in the Yellow Pages or write us for nearest location.

Mileage is based on CUNA Standards. Yours may vary. Check with your Vespa dealer. Wear helmet and eye protection. Check local laws. Vespa of America, 355 Valley Drive, Brisbane, CA 94005.

vespa
THE UNCOMMON CARRIER

179

Part three

THE VESPA FAMILY

A three-wheeled Vespa: the Ape

A three-wheeled Vespa: the Ape

While from the early years of its production the Vespa was seen as a means of personal transport, the Ape (pronounced "Ah-pey" and translated as "Bee") was born and developed exclusively as a commercial vehicle. From 1948 onwards, a number of versions were produced, all characterized by the same basic elements that contributed to the success of the original: great functionality and versatility, small displacement and low fuel consumption, easy to drive, excellent carrying capacity, modest purchase price.

The Ape appeared soon after the Vespa; that is to say, in the immediate post-war period when there was an increasing need for an economical means of transporting goods. Its history runs parallel with that of the Vespa and while not enjoying the same "legendary" status as the scooter nor benefiting from similar advertising resources, for decades it has represented a fundamental vehicle in the field of commercial transport. In certain regions of Italy the Ape was known as the "Lapa", while abroad it had very different names. On English-speaking markets, for obvious reasons Ape was dropped in favour of "Vespa Commercial". In France it was called the "Trivespa", in Portugal the "Vespacar" and in Germany the "Vespa Lastenroller". Naturally, the company tried to exploit the well-known Vespa brand as much as possible.

The birth of the Ape

"The Birth of the Ape", by Corradino D'Ascanio, from the *Piaggio Magazine*, February 1949:

We had to fill a gap in the means of post-war utilitarian locomotion, bringing to the market a small displacement delivery vehicle with low fuel consumption, a modest purchase price and low maintenance that would be easy to drive, manoeuvrable in the heaviest city traffic and, above all, suitable, ready and available for home delivery of goods purchased in the shops. These characteristic three-wheeled vehicles are multiplying day by day in Italian cities as not only do they perform their duty of transporting goods from the shops to the homes of the clients, but also act as a highly visible and effective form of publicity for the companies that have adopted them. We are returning, albeit slowly and gradually, to a comfortable lifestyle and clients no longer want to have to leave shops laden with packages but rather today they prefer to give the shopkeeper their address and have their purchases despatched rapidly from the shop itself. Moreover, a home delivery service presupposes a certain frequency of trips from the central zones to the suburbs of the city and the shopkeeper can hardly demand constant physical labour from his deliverymen. Moreover, time is becoming ever more precious and what is saved in fuel and maintenance for an Ape delivery vehicle is lost in the hours taken by a delivery boy making home deliveries by bicycle or on foot. Means of public transport are detested for their incurably poor service and the now chronic overcrowding that puts the goods to be transported at risk.

A three-wheeled Vespa: the Ape

DOPO IL GRANDIOSO SUCCESSO DELLA MOTOLEGGERA "VESPA,, LA S. p. Az. **PIAGGIO & C.** PRESENTA IL VEICOLO

MOTOFURGONE
UTILITARIO

PORTATA : 2 Quintali

VELOCITA': 40 Km. all'ora

PENDENZA : massima superabile 18 %

CONSUMO : 35 ÷ 40 Km. per litro

La circolazione del Motofurgone "Ape,, è regolata dalle stesse norme valevoli per la Motoleggera "Vespa,,

S. A. R. P. I. CONCESSIONARIA ESCLUSIVA PER LA VENDITA
GENOVA - Via Galata, 33

A three-wheeled Vespa: the Ape

The Ape was clearly born out of the Vespa: the engine was the same 125 cc unit and the wheels, handlebar and controls were the same. The rear section instead presented an infinite series of variants: from a pickup to a van, from a canvas cover to a tipping body, while there was also a "people-moving" version initially known as the Giardinetta and then as the Calessino.

While in just a few years, the Vespa became a perfect vehicle for recreational activities, the Ape remained within the sphere of working transport. Advertising was therefore less creative and more concerned with the concrete advantages of the vehicle.

The Ape was used for carrying goods by numerous companies, from one-man outfits to the most successful corporations. All of them would have their name sign-painted on the rear body creating a lively series of mobile advertising hoardings. Among the most famous names were: Sant'Ambroeus (pastries, Milan), Upim (department stores), Motta (cakes and pastries), Negroni (ham and salami).

It was not just with Vespas that enthusiasts undertook adventurous trips around the world. In 1998, the Italians Brovelli and Martino travelled from Lisbon to Beijing with an Ape TM 703: 25 thousand kilometres on roads and desert tracks in the Eurasia Expedition.

The '40s

Ape A

The Ape was introduced in 1948, the A version having a displacement of 125 cc and a loading capacity of 200 kg. Two versions were produced, a pickup and a van. In 1949, these were joined by the Giardinetta series capable of carrying up to two people.

In the early years the emphasis was placed on the Ape's versatility: "the product delivered to the home accelerates the sales process", "the client is no longer the porter for his own purchase", "rapid home delivery revives the pleasure in purchasing", "a client satisfied in just a few minutes will remain faithful for a lifetime."

Images were drawn and were influenced by the style of the *Domenica del Corriere* front pages.

The brakes featured a pedal with hydraulic actuation for the rear wheels and a handlebar lever for the front wheel. There was also a car-like handbrake acting on the differential. The transmission was composed of a differential and two chains. The manual starting lever was located on the driver's right-hand side. The front suspension featured steel springs, while at the rear shock absorbers were combined with torsion bars. The wheels were in pressed steel. The Giardinetta version introduced in 1949 could be used to carry people or bulky goods.

CHI L'ACQUISTA... *non li spende – li guadagna...*

Un cliente accontentato in pochi minuti, vi rimarrà fedele tutta la vita

Il problema delle comunicazioni e dei trasporti assume una importanza vitale per la prosperità dell'industria e del commercio. La Società Piaggio, traendo profitto dalla sua lunga esperienza nel campo dei motori e dai risultati ottenuti con le soluzioni tecniche che hanno assicurato il successo di diffusione della "Vespa", presenta sul mercato il motofurgone "Ape", studiato per i piccoli e rapidi trasporti, e particolarmente adatto, nelle città, per il servizio a domicilio. Eccezionale stabilità, resistenza allo sforzo e facile manovrabilità, anche nel più intenso traffico metropolitano, sono ottenuti, in questo veicolo utilitario, di modesta manutenzione e di economico impiego. L'esercente potrà accontentare con rapidità e sicurezza la clientela, che ogni giorno di più esige il servizio a domicilio, e con l'uso del motofurgone "Ape", allargherà il campo d'azione della propria attività commerciale.

A three-wheeled Vespa: the Ape

CARATTERISTICHE TECNICHE

Motore : a 2 tempi - cilindrata cmc. 125 potenza massima HP. 4 a 4500 giri.

Cambio di marcia : a 4 velocità.

Messa in moto : con leva a mano azionabile dal posto di guida a sinistra.

Raffreddamento : è assicurato a qualsiasi velocità da un ventilatore centrifugo.

Telaio : di lamiera acciaio stampata e saldata elettricamente.

Trasmissione : con differenziale e due catene.

Sospensione : con molle acciaio a spirale per la ruota anteriore ; con barre di torsione ed ammortizzatori per le ruote posteriori.

Ruote : di lamiera, acciaio stampata, con freno a tamburo, intercambiabili tra loro.

Pressione gomme :
per la ruota anteriore $1,2 \div 1,5$ Kg./cm. 2
per le ruote posteriori $1,5 \div 1,8$ Kg./cm. 2

Freni : a pedale, idraulico, sulle ruote posteriori, a mano sulla ruota anteriore e a leva a mano sul differenziale.

Illuminazione : un faro anteriore a due luci e lampadina di posizione, due fanalini laterali ed un fanalino posteriore, l'alimentazione è fatta a mezzo del generatore collegato ad una batteria.

Cassone : di legno con nervature di rinforzo, sponda posteriore ribaltabile.

Lunghezza massima	m. 2,430
Larghezza »	» 1,280
Altezza »	» 0,860
Altezza della sella da terra	» 0,700
Altezza pedana da terra	» 0,150
Raggio minimo sterzata	» 1,885
Carreggiata	» 1,028
Altezza fondo cassone da terra	» 0,500
Dimensioni cassone	m. 1,110 x 1,110
Altezza sponde cassone	m. 0,200
Peso totale a vuoto	Kg. 125

Velocità massima a pieno carico 40 Km. all'ora.

Carico trasportabile   Kg. 200

Pendenza massima superabile a pieno carico 18 %.

Consumo a pieno carico ; 1 litro di miscela ogni 35 Km.

The '50s

Ape B
Ape C
Ape D

The B version of the Ape appeared in 1953 and boasted an increased displacement of 150 cc and a 300 kg loading capacity.

The C version was introduced in 1956 and featured a 150 cc engine and pressed-steel bodywork. There was also a proper seat (rather than a saddle) for the driver, a reverse gear and electric starting. The loading capacity rose to 350 kg. Pickup, van and calesse or rickshaw versions were available. The D series was introduced in 1958 with the same range of versions.

A vast range of models and versions was offered. Emphasis was placed on the Ape's potential as a capacious and efficient means of transportation in every situation and climatic condition. Piaggio also tried to encourage sales by offering hire purchase schemes.

The early Ape models enjoyed great commercial success: in the first ten years no less than 200,000 examples were delivered. In 1960, on the occasion of the Olympic Games in Rome, it was used as an official vehicle within the Olympic Village. The Ape became an increasingly common sight in the large cities and many small businesses enjoyed excellent service from Piaggio's small three-wheeler.

A three-wheeled Vespa: the Ape

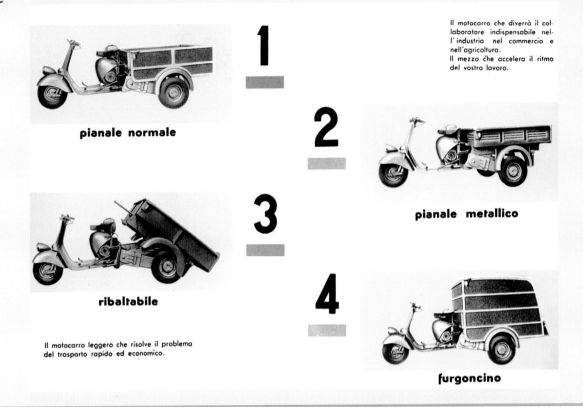

1 pianale normale

Il motocarro che diverrà il collaboratore indispensabile nell'industria nel commercio e nell'agricoltura.
Il mezzo che accelera il ritmo del vostro lavoro.

2 pianale metallico

3 ribaltabile

Il motocarro leggero che risolve il problema del trasporto rapido ed economico.

4 furgoncino

The '60s

Pentarò
Ape MP

With the Pentarò 250 of 1961 the Ape doubled up: a separate rear trailer with two wheels was added to the three-wheeled motorized unit. This led to a two-fold increase in loading capacity to 700 kg.

The Pentarò was a small articulated vehicle with a front three-wheeled tractor unit and a rear trailer on a pair of stabilising wheels. The tractor had the same form as the Ape while the semi-trailer could be unhooked as with large trucks. With the Pentarò, Piaggio ventured into a new area of the light transport sector with a practical, relatively economical and highly original vehicle.

1966 saw a significant technical innovation with the introduction of the MP ("motore posteriore" or rear engine) 190: direct transmission to the rear half shafts provided significantly improved traction. The cabin was radically modified and more comfortable. Pickup, van, calesse or rickshaw and tipping versions were available. The loading capacity rose to 550 kg. The MPV version appeared in 1968 and featured a steering wheel rather than handlebars.

The success achieved with well-known companies encouraged Piaggio to publicize images of the Apes used by its clients. The slogan claimed: "The vehicle for you is the Ape, because the Ape produces, because the Ape helps you earn."

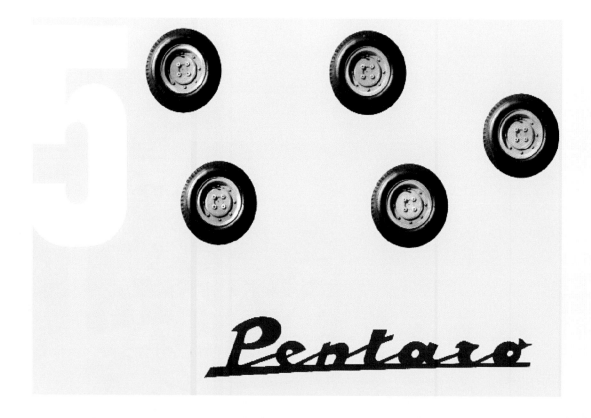

A three-wheeled Vespa: the Ape

Part three

THE VESPA FAMILY

A four-wheeled Vespa: the 400

A four-wheeled Vespa: the 400

The Vespa 400 was designed and developed by Piaggio entirely in-house. However, Fiat, which supplied the sheet metal to Pontedera (and above all had a 96% share of all cars on the road in Italy), did not view this new utility car favourably. This was partly due to the fact that it was presented in 1957, just four months from the launch of the Fiat 500. Nonetheless it made its debut at the Paris Motor Show, with an exceptional product endorser: Juan Manuel Fangio. Production was started by the French company ACMA in its factory at Fourchambault. The car faced competition in France from the Citroën 2CV and the Renault 4CV, although they cost between 10 and 15% more. They did, however, have the advantage of carrying four people while the Vespa 400 had only room for two. Among the advantages of the 400 were good roadholding and the spaciousness of the cabin.

The engine was an air-cooled two-stroke twin with a displacement of exactly 393 cc. The power unit was rear mounted and drove the rear wheels. Independent suspension was fitted all round along with four-wheel hydraulic brakes. With a total length of 2.83 metres the Vespa 400 weighed just 360 kg. Fuel consumption: 5 litres of oil/fuel blend/100 km. The Vespa 400 was reasonably successful: 30,000 examples were produced between 1957 and 1961, only around a hundred of which arrived in Italy.

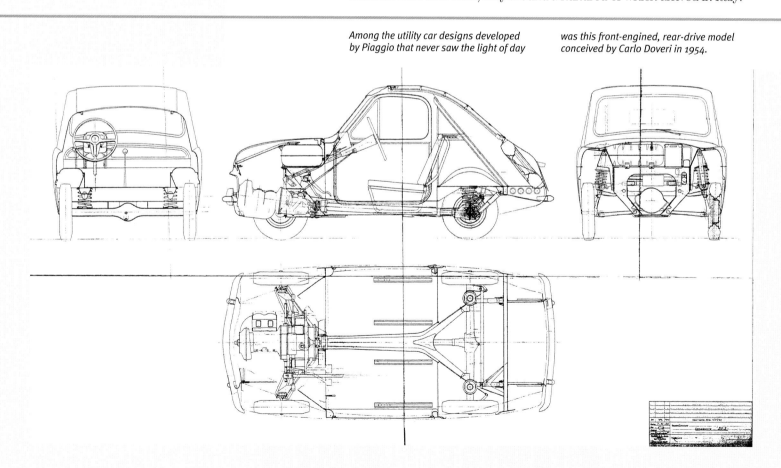

Among the utility car designs developed by Piaggio that never saw the light of day was this front-engined, rear-drive model conceived by Carlo Doveri in 1954.

A four-wheeled Vespa: the 400

The Vespa 400 and expeditions

As with the Vespa, there were clients eager to demonstrate the reliability of the 400 over long distances. In the August of 1958, Raymond Miomandre and René Pari completed a return trip from Paris to Moscow: 7000 kilometres in 140 hours, without any mechanical repairs being required. Four Vespa 400s entered and completed the gruelling Monte Carlo Rally, confirming the four-wheeled Vespa's great reliability.

A cutaway view of the Vespa 400 published in advance by the French press early in 1957.

Note the engine-transmission assembly, the fully independent suspension and the spare wheel behind the seat.

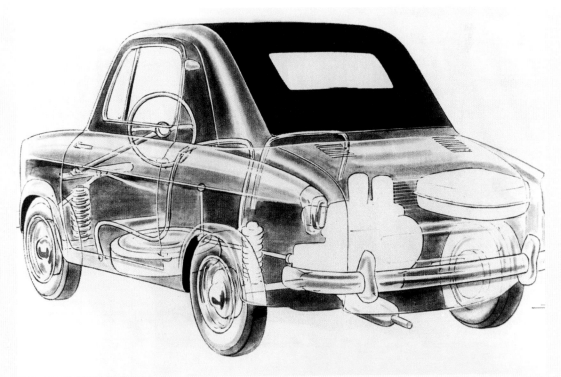

A four-wheeled Vespa: the 400

la plus pratique... la moins chère!

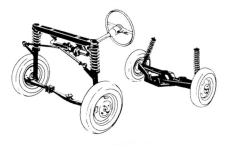

MANIABILITÉ : Le rayon de braquage de la VESPA 400, de
3 m 80, et l'encombrement réduit de la voiture permettent
de se garer dans l'emplacement minimum.

BEAUTÉ DES LIGNES

La VESPA 400 est la voiture
de l'actualité. Consomma-
tion, garage, assurances,
entretien la rendent im-
battable sur le plan économique.

Mais si elle est une voi-
ture économique, la VESPA
400, ne le sacrifie en rien
à la beauté des lignes et à
l'élégance.

Alliant l'habitabilité et le
confort à une recherche
d'esthétique très poussée,
la VESPA 400 est une
"2 CV racée" aussi agréable
pour le travail et les voya-
ges, que pour les courses
en ville d'une femme élé-
gante.

A four-wheeled Vespa: the 400

La nouvelle VESPA 400 modèle 1960 présente toute une gamme de perfectionnements fort appréciables.

Un soin tout spécial a été apporté à son aménagement intérieur : sièges confortables, poches de portières, glaces de côté coulissantes, moteur beaucoup plus silencieux.

Les nouveaux coloris de sa carrosserie sont jeunes et variés.

Son moteur est garanti 50.000 km ou 2 ans, quelle assurance pour vous et quelle économie !

En ville vous ne pourrez plus vous en passer, à la campagne elle vous rendra de grands services.

Elle vous plaira par son élégance, son confort, sa rapidité et son extrême robustesse.

Vous, *Madame*, vous serez séduite par ses lignes, son élégance complétera la vôtre, elle augmentera la personnalité de votre charme.

Vous, *Monsieur*, vous apprécierez sa nervosité, sa tenue de route, sa maniabilité, son économie, et son faible encombrement.

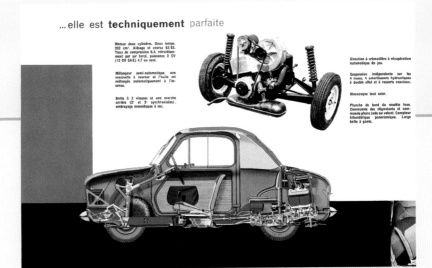

...elle est **techniquement** parfaite

Moteur deux cylindres. Deux temps, 393 cm³. Alésage et course 63.63. Taux de compression 6,4, refroidissement par air forcé, puissance 2 CV (12 CV SAE) 4.7 au cent.

Mélangeur semi-automatique, une manivelle à tourner et l'huile est mélangée automatiquement à l'essence.

Boîte à 3 vitesses et une marche arrière (2ᵉ et 3ᵉ synchronisées), embrayage monodisque à sec.

Direction à crémaillère à récupération automatique du jeu.

Suspension indépendante sur les 4 roues, 4 amortisseurs hydrauliques à double effet à ressorts coaxiaux.

Monocoque tout acier.

Planche de bord du modèle luxe. Commande des clignotants et commande phare code au volant. Compteur kilométrique panoramique. Large boîte à gants.

vive • élégante • sobre • pratique • agréable •

Capote s'ouvrant facilement. Vitres de côté coulissantes. Déflecteurs. Voie avant 1,760 m. voie arrière 1,160 m. empattement 1,690 m. largeur hors tout 1,27 m. longueur hors tout 2,85 m. hauteur totale à vide 1,25 m. poids à vide 360 kg.

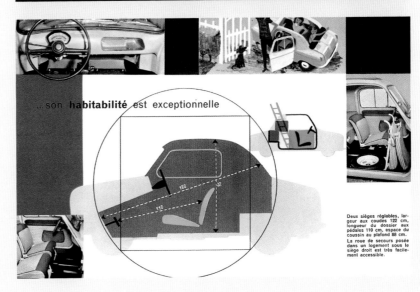

... son **habitabilité** est exceptionnelle

Deux sièges réglables, largeur aux coudes 122 cm, longueur du dossier aux pédales 110 cm, espace du coussin au plafond 88 cm.

La roue de secours posée dans un logement sous le siège droit est très facilement accessible.

THE VESPA FAMILY

An outboard Vespa:
the Moscone

An outboard Vespa: the Moscone

The Moscone (or Fly in English) completed the insect trio initiated with the Vespa and the Ape. It was, in fact, an outboard engine introduced by Piaggio in 1949 with the intention of making motor boating accessible to all. In Piaggio advertising, the Moscone was always photographed against highly attractive marine backdrops with the possibility of reaching these locations in a particularly economical manner. In the case of the Moscone too, albeit to a much lesser degree than with the Vespa, recourse was made to the world of actresses, in this case with Rossana Podestà.

"Moscone, the Long-Awaited Outboard", from the *Piaggio Magazine*, by Vincenzo Balsamo, pioneer of Italian motor boating, navy officer and Vice President of the FIM:

The development and spread of the outboard engine in practical use; that is to say in the application of the marine power unit for recreational or utilitarian purposes has not followed that rising path it was logical to expect as a consequence of the sparkling results achieved in sporting competition. Within the complex technical and economical phenomenon of the spread of the means of locomotion on water, a need was felt to tend

An outboard Vespa: the Moscone

towards an engine with a very small displacement only from which could derive the required conditions for the popularity of the outboard engine. In other words, a large sector of the public needed to be put in the position of being able to own a motorboat that was easy and safe to use, of modest speed and with running costs accessible to the all.

A decisive step with wide repercussions for the outboard sector was taken in 1949 with the appearance of a concrete proposal from the Italian industry. This was not a one-off still at the experimental stage, but rather an engine with a displacement of just 100 cc that had already passed all the most severe tests and that entered the vast panorama of national and inter-national motor boating as a factor of undoubted value for its expansion. The "Moscone" that has recently emerged from the Piaggio workshops embraces those prerequisites of an engine that wishes to be defined as utilitarian: materials carefully selected for their physical and mechanical properties, ingen-ious and practical controls, ease of starting, protection of the immersed components and the vital organs from the action of the water, lightness and robustness of the assembly, simplicity

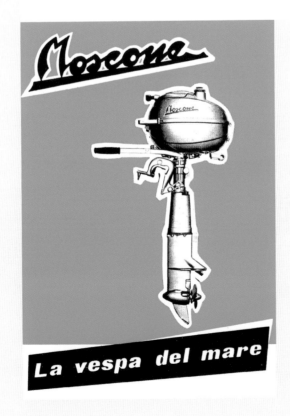

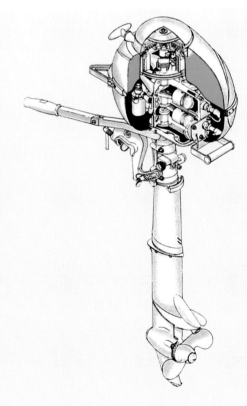

An outboard Vespa: the Moscone

of application to any boat. The engine is a twin-cylinder two-stroke unit and develops 3.3 brake horsepower at 4000 rpm. Ignition is via a flywheel-magneto with special magnets, with coils, condenser and contact breaker for the alternate firing of the two cylinders; the cables and sparkplugs are suitably waterproofed. The unit is started with an automatic recoil cord and is water-cooled with a self-priming and self-adjusting pump.

The propeller is made of a special non-corroding aluminium-magnesium alloy, reverse is immediate through the rotation of the motor and the underwater exhaust ensures the unit runs quietly. The overall weight of the motor is just 17 kg. With this compact mechanical jewel, enclosed in a compact volume, with harmonically tapering lines in an elegant fairing, attached to an ordinary boat one may attain speeds varying from 2.5 to 12 kph and a range of 3.3 hours at cruising speed or 2 hours at maximum speed. It therefore provides the opportunity to undertake the kind of nautical cruising to which many aspire but have until now found the economic factor to be the greatest obstacle and limitation.

The Piaggio boatyard also presented an elegant clinker-built wooden boat on the occasion of the launch of the Moscone outboard motor.

Part four

COMMUNICATION

Publicizing the Vespa

The '40s

In the early years of production, Piaggio concentrated on the novelty value of the Vespa.

The first full-page advertisement simply read: «Piaggio & C. S.p.A. presents the Vespa light motorcycle.»

Subsequently there was a deliberate attempt to characterize the Vespa as a product far removed from the traditional image of the two-wheeled vehicles of the time. Parallels were instead drawn with the comfort of the car: «Not a motorcycle, but rather a small two-wheeled car.» The copy emphasized the greater protection offered by the Vespa with respect to motorcycles: «You may continue to use it through the winters as you are protected from mud and you may travel swiftly, safely and comfortably without soiling your clothes with engine oil or dust from the road.» All this in great safety «guaranteed on wet and slippery roads thanks to exceptional stability.»

The financial resources of the potential clients were relatively modest in this period and Piaggio encouraged sales by offering the enticement of instalment plans. The advertising therefore avoided the superfluous and focussed on very concrete features. In this phase the Vespa represented not so much a recreational vehicle as a means of getting to work.

Alla fine della stagione estiva **si consideri** che la Vespa 125 cmc. a molleggio integrale

non è una motocicletta ma piuttosto

« una piccola vettura a due ruote »

che si può **continuare** ad usare nella stagione invernale perchè si è riparati dal fango e assicurati sulle strade bagnate e viscide da una stabilità eccezionale.

Con la **«Vespa»** si viaggia rapidi, sicuri e confortevolmente, senza sporcarsi i vestiti con l'olio del motore e la polvere della strada.

Gomme **PIRELLI**

S. p. A. PIAGGIO & C. - Genova
FILIALE DI MILANO: Via Pallavicino 31 - Tel. 43.900 - FILIALE DI TORINO: C.so Unione Sovietica 43 - Tel. 682.396
AGENTI DI VENDITA IN TUTTA ITALIA

UN NUOVO PRODOTTO PIAGGIO:

Il motocarrozzino per la *Vespa*

razionalmente studiato
nell' **ATTACCO**
nel **PESO**
nella **FORMA**

Gomme **PIRELLI**   PREZZO COMPLETO L. 52.000
(FRANCO FABBRICA)

S.p.A. PIAGGIO & C. - Genova
FILIALE DI MILANO: Via Pallavicino 31 - Tel. 43.900 - FILIALE DI TORINO: C.so Unione Sovietica 43 - Tel. 682.396
Agenti di vendita in tutta Italia

Vespa

La motoleggera veramente utilitaria realizzata dalla **Soc. p. a. Piaggio & C.**

Motore a due tempi
Cilindrata cmc. 98
Cambio a 3 velocità
Velocità 60 km. l'ora
Pendenza superabile 20%
Consumo 50 km. con 1 litro

ELENCO DEI CONCESSIONARI

LAZIO
DI GENNARO Luigi - Roma - Via del Clementino, n. 92-93 - Tel. 63.151.

PIEMONTE
B.T.F. - Torino, Corso Tortona, 12 - Tel .80.625.

LOMBARDIA
GHIZZONI OSVALDO - Milano, Via Paolo Sarpi, 53 - Tel. 91-768.

LIGURIA
SOC. « LA MOTO » - Genova, Viale Brigate Partigiane, 56 - Tel. 51.307.

TOSCANA
MOTORAB - Firenze, Via G. B. Lulli, 2 - Tel. 21-094.

VENEZIA EUGANEA E TRIDENTINA
MARSENGO BASTIA FILIPPO - Padova, Via Verdi, 4 - Tel. 22.668.

VENEZIA GIULIA
ROTI RODOLFO - Trieste, Via S. Francesco, 46 - Tel. 85-28.

EMILIA ORIENTALE
C.IB. - Bologna, Via De' Mussolini, 1

EMILIA OCCIDENTALE
GELMINI ALESSIO - Parma, Strada Vitt. Emanuele, 41 - Tel. 41-71.

MARCHE
S.E.R.T.A. - Ancona, Strada Vecchini a Borgorodi, 1 - Tel. 38-32.

UMBRIA
S.E.R.T.A. - Perugia, Corso Vannucci, 23.

CALABRIA
DE DOMENICO PASQUALE - Bovalino Marina (R C.)

PENISOLA SALENTINA
BARDICCHIA FRANCESCO - Lecce, Via Ammirati, n. 26 - Tel. 12-10.

ABRUZZI
BESLTER. - Pescara, Corso Vitt. Eman. 152.

SICILIA
AGRIFOGLIO dr. POMPEO - Palermo, Via Dante, 58 - Tel. 17-981.

CAMPANIA E LUCANIA
R.I.C. - Rappresentanze Industriali e Commerciali S.A.R.L. - Napoli, Via Carlo Poerio, 79.

RAPPRESENTANTE GENERALE PER LA VENDITA :

S.A.R.P.I. - Via Galata, 33 - Telefono 54.770 - GENOVA

The '50s

At this point the Vespa's success was assured, but Piaggio's advertising continued to claim that it was the «smallest two-wheeled car» and that «better a Vespa today than a car tomorrow», so as not to confuse it with motorcycles. The qualities of the Vespa were emphasized as a means of competing with the rivals that began to appear in the wake of the Piaggio scooter's success: «the most widely-used scooter», «a product of quality», «the most comprehensive after-sale service». In order to attract a female clientele, the Vespa was frequently portrayed with girls alongside. Rather than a utiliatrian means of transport, it became a consumer good. Hence the exhortation «Vespizzatevi!» or «Vesparize yourselves!».

In this period, the general public began to enjoy greater economic resources; the "economic miracle" was in full swing and a clientele that could look upon the Vespa as a recreational vehicle had to be captured. People were perhaps now inclined to permit themselves a meal in a restaurant out of town, something unthinkable just a few years earlier. The marketing idiom changed accordingly as Piaggio turned to a broader clientele eager to shrug off the deprivations of the post-war years. However, the firm also had to defend itself against its first competitors: the Lambretta was not the only threat as by now all the motorcycle manufacturers had a scooter in their range.

*Quando
sarò grande
andrò in
VESPA*

Tra trent'anni

*In Vespa

ci si ama meglio*

The '60s

Maybe your second car shouldn't be a car.

By now the Vespa was extremely popular and advertising began to emphasize its international success «throughout the world». The problem of traffic began to make itself felt, but with the Vespa this was «not a problem», «with the Vespa you're always on time». However, towards the end of the '60s, there was an increasingly powerful current of change stemming from the world's youth movements. These were the years of protest, long hair and miniskirts, the music of the Beatles and rebellious behaviour.

While previously, Piaggio's advertising campaigns had been fairly traditional, the late Sixties saw a sharp break with the past as the company decided to ride the revolutionary wave sweeping through the period. The Vespa was by now an established product and the advertising idiom could therefore become more creative, with highly innovative images and slogans. The years in which the Vespa served essentially as an economical means of travelling to work were long past. Other demands now had to be met and Piaggio tackled the period with advertising campaigns of great impact: a bold use of colour, attractive images and even daring poses with beautiful girls.

con la *Vespa* non e' un problema

lo scooter più venduto nel mondo

con la *Vespa* non e' un problema

The '70s

The historic slogan «Chi Vespa mangia le mele» (usually translated as «Who Vespas eats the apples») came out of this period. Piaggio exploited the success of the earlier campaigns with the slogan «Mela compro la Vespa», a play on words with Mela meaning both "apple" and "I'll… it", the slogan translating literally as "I'll buy it, the Vespa" and more idiomatically as "I'm getting a Vespa". However, the period also saw the rise of an ecologist movement, with pollution, above all in relation to cars, being discussed for the first time. A new campaign was created and here again there was a play on words: the invented term "sardomobili" associated cars stuck in traffic with sardines crammed into tins. «Sardomobili steal the air», «Sardomobili don't love others». Naturally, the Vespa instead offered freedom and happiness: «Enjoy Vespa!», «Who Vespas shines». In America a slogan suggested that «Perhaps your next car shouldn't be a car».

gIOiati Vespa

esci dal guscio

PIAGGIO cambia il mondo in due ruote

Nuova Vespa 125 TS.

esci dal guscio

gIOiati Vespa

PIAGGIO cambia il mondo in due ruote

Chi Vespa mangia le mele

How did this successful slogan come about? The powers that be at Pontedera courageously decided to back a new advertising campaign that would reflect the period of great changes. The language was completely new and the style reflected the Pop Art of those years. There was considerable resistance to the campaign at first but it eventually appeared in the press, on posters and in the sales outlets with unprecedented coverage. «Who Vespas eats the apples» was taken up by the media and transcended the two-wheeled world to enter the collective consciousness. Umberto Eco and Oliviero Toscani talked about it in *L'Espresso* and Luca di Montezemolo did likewise in *Storia Illustrata*.

Filippetti of the Leader agency of Florence explains how the campaign was born:
That day I was on my way back to the agency after lunch, impregnated and soaked by the rain of stimuli coming from all directions. I was looking out of the bus, thinking about the new Vespa campaign on which I was working. As the driver suddenly braked, someone said, «here we go, the usual hassle with rowdy students on the march!». The whistles of the first smoke bombs and the sirens of the arriving Jeeps were in the air. Sitting down and protected from the smoke, I saw him from the window. Calm, impassive, taking no notice of the chaos around him, an apple gripped between his teeth he painted in white letters on the wall: «Trust no one over thirty.» Stunning. A new, unheard of commandment. Words used as weapons that gunned down half the people on the bus and left me with the sensation that with an idea like that, with those words, an era of passion was about to begin.
Back at the agency I looked at the blank sheet of paper in front on me, reflecting on those words, on that idea. I felt a great urge to recount that new reality for Vespa, with the language that it was itself constructing. «Who Vespas yes, who doesn't Vespa no». The pen was writing by itself: Variant A: «Who Vespas touches the sun, who doesn't Vespa no». Variant B: «Who Vespas eats the apples, who doesn't Vespa no». That's it! Found it! Yes, that kid would have painted a phrase like this, that's all, cool. I called Pico Tamburini, head of the Leader agency, and he said, «Fine Gib! Fresh as rainwater! It'll be hell to sell though.» I could already hear them, the "those that don't" coming to blows with the "those that do" during the
presentation, bickering amongst themselves: «But why an apple?», «transgression and freshness, sir.» «But we sell Vespas!», «Good eaters, Mr President.» «But what about this strange slogan…?» «We're selling to eighteen-year-olds, boss.» And the worst of them: «But who's paying? The agricultural board? Come on, Zancani, call Fillippetti at Leader, get him to correct the grammar at least. Put a nice verb after the noun, sweeten the phrase, it'll be less traumatic!»
The great Dr. Zancani, then the director of the publicity department at Genoa. He caught on to that campaign right away, and like a true Sessantottino [a participant in the 1968 protest movement] managed to impose it on the powers that be. «A very dangerous idea» said the tests, but he decided that there had to be a Piaggio contribution to the revolution of joy, a corporate way of sharing with the kids the power of imagination.
All sorts were said, but it was also immediately spoken of as a landmark campaign. «Who Vespas» became part of the collective consciousness.
From time to time I ask myself what and where he is now, that kid painting words as weapons on the walls. By now, he too will be one of "those that don't". I see him still riding fast on a Vespa, not telling anyone that the secret of his eternal youth is that "who Vespas yes".

Publicizing the Vespa

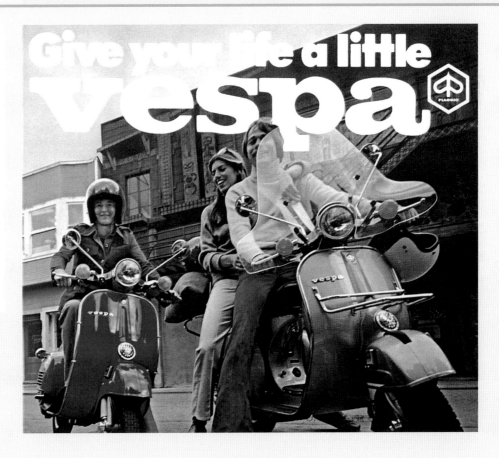

The '80s

While less revolutionary with respect to the previous decades, the advertising campaigns in this period played with language and emphasized the freedom of wide, open spaces. «Today I'm the sea», «Today I'm the woods», «I Vespa, you Jane». The copy also highlighted the Vespisti's sense of initiative and efficiency: "Vespa: moves the will to get things done», «Vespa: changes things».

To celebrate Italy's triumph in the 1982 World Cup the patriotic slogan read, «L'Italia s'è Vespa!», a play on the second line of the national anthem «L'Italia s'è desta», «Italy has awakened.»

The advertising in this period was less incisive, more tentative. On the one hand there was the market composed of young and trendy consumers while on the other there was a more mature clientele in search of sophisticated user-friendly products.

Piaggio appealed to the younger generations above all through the advertising campaign that early in the year cited Marx rather than March, while it offered the Automatica to the adults with the slogan «From here to there easily».

In general, all the proposals show how much attention Piaggio paid to communications with Pontedera always careful to evaluate everything that was going on around it, from politics through to social themes.

L'Italia s'è !

NUOVE VESPA PK 50 E 125
L'ITALIA S'E' VESPA

Nuove VESPA PK: quattro modelli, tre motori e decine di innovazioni tecniche ed estetiche.
Nuove VESPA PK: una linea compatta tutta in acciaio che conquista un nuovo primato di styling. Le nuove VESPA PK sono docili nei comandi, brillanti nella ripresa, decise in frenata, sicure e confortevoli nella guida. Sono dotate di serie di accensione elettronica, lampeggiatori, bauletto porta oggetti, alloggiamento ruota di scorta, unica chiave che comanda accensione e bloccasterzo.

LE NUOVE VESPA PK 50 ELECTRONIC, PK 50 S ELECTRONIC, PK 125 ELECTRONIC, PK 125 S ELECTRONIC 3 CON CILINDRO A TRE TRAVASI, SI AFFIANCANO ALLA GAMMA DELLE VESPA PX PER RIPETERNE IL SUCCESSO E APRIRE UN NUOVO CAPITOLO NELLA STORIA DELLO SCOOTER.

PIAGGIO

The '90s

The early part of the decade was devoted to the problematic launch of the Cosa. From plays on words, «Quella Cosa della Piaggio» («Piaggio's Thing»), «Che Cosa la vita» («What a Thing is life») the campaign moved on to technological aspects: «It has an anti-lock braking circuit but it's not a Mercedes. What is it?» Fortunately, in 1996, the firm moved on to the celebrations for the 50th anniversary of the Vespa and attention was naturally focussed on the brand-new ET4: «It's great to think with your own Vespa!»

The PX was given no advertising support, the intention being to let it gradually fade away from the Piaggio catalogue. It was its clientele that ensured its career continued despite the absence of commercial backing. Low-key campaigns were also run for the small 50 and 125 models that were not very different to their counterparts from the previous decade and therefore difficult to promote with any great enthusiasm.

Scansati baloccone

Per VESPA 50 lo stile non è solo un fatto estetico, non è un optional.
È il frutto di un design razionale, il punto di arrivo di una evoluzione che solo una grande azienda come

Piaggio può permettersi.
VESPA 50 si differenzia da tutto e da tutti per tre caratteristiche che la rendono unica:
□ le marce, per una guida in grado di dare sempre

una interpretazione personale della strada
□ la carrozzeria autoportante, stampata in un solo blocco, che porta con sé un concetto rivoluzionario per il mondo del due ruote

□ l'acciaio con cui è costruita, certezza di solidità e sicurezza di guida in ogni circostanza.
Perché VESPA 50 è un mito che resta.

vespa 50 gelosia d'acciaio con tre marce   PIAGGIO

Ha il circuito frenante antibloccaggio ma non è una Mercedes. Cos'è?

E' l'unico scooter dotato, a richiesta, del sistema frenante EBC (Electronic Brake Control) che modula la pressione del circuito frenante impedendo il bloccaggio della ruota anteriore e assicurando una frenata efficace e modulare anche alle alte velocità. E' nuovo in tutto.

La sella è lunga e larga, le sospensioni calibrate, la strumentazione tra le più moderne. E' la Nuova Cosa Piaggio. E in più, i clienti Cosa potranno usufruire di un Numero Verde per qualsiasi osservazione legata all'utilizzo del veicolo.

La Nuova Cosa.
PIAGGIO

The 2000s

The advertising campaign focussing on the new four-stroke ET4 models that carried the Vespa into the new millennium began in the late Nineties. Pride in the new creation was obvious: «It's great thinking with your own Vespa», with Vespa rhyming with the Italian word "testa" meaning head. It was in these years that the internet became such an all-important part of our lives and the Vespa could even be ordered from the website. The advertising campaign featured the full-page slogan «Download is complete», while alongside a satisfied girl in front of a computer «has just bought her new Vespa between a brioche and a coffee» without even having to visit a dealer. The scooter's strong personality shines through in the campaigns for the successive LX: «Enjoy it» and «Mistreat it». The relative images were painstakingly composed from the points of view of setting and illumination, with a touch of irony provided by the presence of the subjects: in the female version there is an acrobat while in the male image there is a disturbing figure armed with a whip. Poetry and irony instead appeared in the advertising campaign for the Granturismo series: «Even the wind enjoys a caress» and «At 59 you can do without plastic», a play on words and a gentle dig at the other scooters on the market without the benefit of a steel monocoque.

The 2010s

In the 2010s the Vespa has been seen above all outside the usual advertising pages. There have been numerous Italian products of the most diverse kinds that have used the celebrated scooters from Pontedera, both classics and current models, in their advertising campaigns as testimonials emphasising their "Made in Italy" appeal. In what has been a new development of recent years, the Vespa has also appeared in window displays, both in Italy and abroad. Here too, it would be hard to find anything better if you are trying to communicate "Italian-ness" through the display of a single iconic object. Vespa: the legend in the legend.

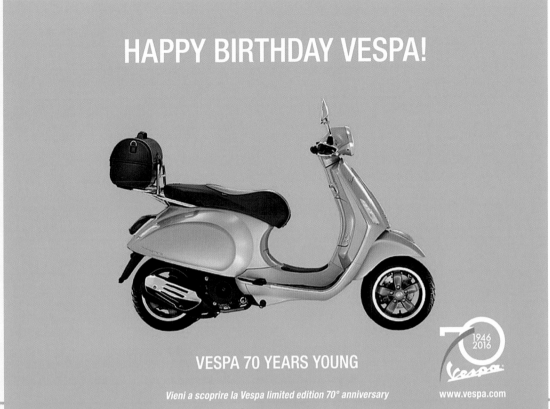

Publicizing the Vespa

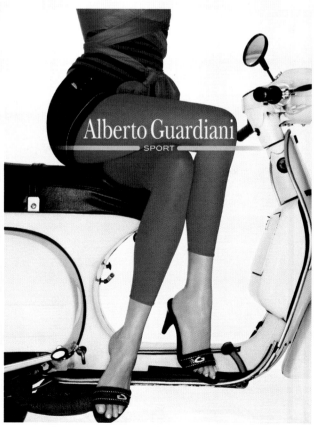

Publicizing the Vespa

Top case. 38 lt. di capacità e la possibilità di accessori vari e schienalino specifico per far viaggiare comodamente anche il tuo passeggero.

Soft Bags. Due borse laterali da moto e scooter provviste di una comoda tasca termica per le vivande.

Monospalla. Il pratico zaino che diventa marsupio, dotato anche del passaggio per il cavo del tuo lettore mp3.

Top case. 47 lt di capacità da abbinare se lo vuoi a un kit di luci di stop per viaggiare in massima sicurezza.

Bella in vista: la Kappa scooterista.

Gli accessori giusti per attraversare la città sono KAPPA!

Pratici per il tuo scooter o la tua moto, affidabili e sempre di moda. Zaini monospalla, valigie e borse morbide con il design più accattivante al miglior rapporto qualità-prezzo. Scegli uno stile metropolitano con la massima sicurezza su strada.

Vai su www.kappamoto.com e scopri la nuova linea di accessori!
KAPPA S.r.l. - info@kappamoto.com

KAPPA

www.cafenoir.it

CAFèNOIR
SHOES. BAGS AND ACCESSORIES

Publicizing the Vespa

La Dolce Vita

Bella Italia. You can't describe the name of any other country as flatteringly as you can Italy. And rightly so. Not only does the country ensnare its guests with imposing mountain peaks and apparently endless beaches, it's also packed full of countless historical art treasures. Italy also display first-class taste in fashion, lifestyle and of course its famous cuisine.

Discover the beauty of Italy for yourself – we've put together some great package deals with our partners for you here.

Search by country
Italy

SiXT rent a car

A voyage of discovery
How about spending your next holiday touring Tuscany with a Sixt rental car? You can redeem your miles online with Sixt for a car of your choice. You are free to choose the rental period and destination. Cars can also be booked at short notice. www.sixt.com/lufthansa

Available from 7,500 miles

G·T·A
PANTALONI

Publicizing the Vespa

Part four

COMMUNICATION

The Piaggio Calendar

The Calendar

When it first came out it caused a sensation with a certain bishop actually declaring that it was pornographic. In effect, from the outset the Piaggio calendar emphasised the combination of Vespa and beautiful women, the latter usually being scantily clad. It was hardly surprising that in the Fifties this created something of a scandal. In any case, it has to be admitted that Piaggio had a good eye: many of the girls photographed went on to become famous models or actresses.

The first Piaggio calendar appeared in 1951. The girls were portrayed in splendid drawings inspired by the covers of the most popular Italian periodicals of the era such as the *Domenica del Corriere* or *Grand Hotel*. From 1951 to 1954, the drawings were executed by the celebrated Franco Mosca. From 1955 onwards, the girls instead appeared in photographs. Each edition was based on a different theme, from travel (1951) to sport (1952), from nature to animals… In 1957, the girls and their Vespas were superimposed over drawings, while in 1959 the background was black in order to lend greater emphasis to the subjects.

During the Fifties, Leo Longanesi produced some stunning drawings depicting Vespas with a highly original and particularly sophisticated style.

The Piaggio Calendar

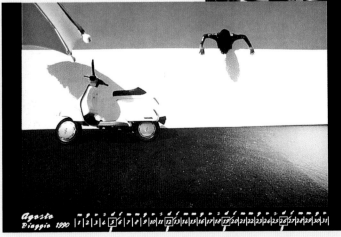

The '50s

gennaio

D	5	12	19	26
L	6	13	20	27
M	7	14	21	28
M	1	8	15	22	29
G	2	9	16	23	30
V	3	10	17	24	31
S	4	11	18	25

agosto

D	1	8	15	22	29
L	2	9	16	23	30
M	3	10	17	24	31
M	4	11	18	25
G	5	12	19	26
V	6	13	20	27
S	7	14	21	28

mayo

D	L	M	M	J	V	S
1	2	3	4	5	6	7
8	9	10	11	12	13	14
15	16	17	18	19	20	21
22	23	24	25	26	27	28
29	30	31

luglio

D	1	8	15	22	29
L	2	9	16	23	30
M	3	10	17	24	31
M	4	11	18	25
		12	19	26
		13	20	27
		14	21	28

ottobre

D		7	14	21	28
L	1	8	15	22	29
M	2	9	16	23	30
M	3	10	17	24	31
G	4	11	18	25
V	5	12	19	26
S	6	13	20	27

marzo

D	L	M	M	J	V	S
					1	2
3	4	5	6	7	8	9
10	11	12	13	14	15	16
17	18	19	20	21	22	23
24 31	25	26	27	28	29	30

julio

D	L	M	M	J	V	S
	1	2	3	4	5	6
7	8	9	10	11	12	13
14	15	16	17	18	19	20
21	22	23	24	25	26	27
28	29	30	31			

The '60s

DICEMBRE

D	L	M	M	G	V	S
					1	2	3
						9	10
						16	17
						23	24
						30	31

D	L
3	4
10	11
17	18
24	25

LUGLIO

D	L	M	M	G	V	S
					1	2
3	4	5	6	7	8	9
10	11	12	13	14	15	16
17	18	19	20	21	22	23
24 31	25	26	27	28	29	30

APRILE

D	L	M	M	G	V	S
						1
2	3	4	5	6	7	8
9	10	11	12	13	14	15
16	17	18	19	20	21	22
23 30	24	25	26	27	28	29

GIUGNO

D	L	M	M	G	V	S
				1	2	3
4	5	6	7	8	9	10
11	12	13	14	15	16	17
18	19	20	21	22	23	24
25	26	27	28	29	30	

FEBBRAIO

D	L	M	M	G	V	S
	1	2	3	4	5	6
7	8	9	10	11	12	13
14	15	16	17	18	19	20
21	22	23	24	25	26	27
28	29					

The Piaggio Calendar

NOVEMBRE

D	L	M	M	G	V	S
					1	2
3	4	5	6	7	8	9
10	11	12	13	14	15	16
17	18	19	20	21	22	23
24	25	26	27	28	29	30

FEBRUAR

S	M	D	M	D	F	S
				1	2	3
4	5	6	7	8	9	10
11	12	13	14	15	16	17
18	19	20	21	22	23	24
25	26	27	28			

MÄRZ

S	M	D	M	D	F	S
				1	2	3
4	5	6	7	8	9	10
11	12	13	14	15	16	17
18	19	20	21	22	23	24
25	26	27	28	29	30	31

APRILE

D	L	M	M	G	V	S
	1	2	3	4	5	6
7	8	9	10	11	12	13
14	15	16	17	18	19	20
21	22	23	24	25	26	27
28	29	30				

Models and actresses

the italians

Raffaella Carrà	May 1966
Sylva Koscina	February 1962
Antonella Lualdi	October 1963
Elsa Martinelli	January 1964
Sandra Milo	July 1964
Giorgia Moll	March 1964
Luciana Paluzzi	February 1966
Paola Pitagora	October 1966
Silvana Podestà	March 1962
Stefania Sandrelli	March 1964
Daniela Rocca	September 1963
Catherine Spaak	March1963
Marilù Tolo	September 1965
Ornella Vanoni	November 1962
Serena Vergano	August 1965

foreign stars

Elga Andersen	January 1966
Ursula Andress	January 1965
Claudine Auger	August 1967
Caroll Baker	September 1963
Geraldine Chaplin	May 1967
Cyd Charisse	October 1967
Joan Collins	December 1966
Mireille Darc	December 1960
Sandra Dee	August 1964
Mylene Demongeot	November 1963
Angie Dickinson	January 1963
Britt Ekland	April 1966
Anna Maria Ferrero	September 1962
Alice & Ellen Kessler	June 1964
Dalhia Lavi	December 1964
Margaret Lee	July 1966
Jayne Mansfield	November 1964
Michele Mercier	May 1964
Pascale Petit	October 1964
Elke Sommer	February 1964
Agnes Spaak	December 1965
Gloria St. Paul	June 1963
Susan Strasberg	February 1965
Marina Vlady	August 1963
Raquel Welch	August 1967
Joan Whelan	june 1967

The Piaggio Calendar

GIUGNO

D	L	M	M	G	V	S
						1
2	3	4	5	6	7	8
9	10	11	12	13	14	15
16	17	18	19	20	21	22
23/30	24	25	26	27	28	29

MARZO

D	L	M	M	G	V	S
					1	2
3	4	5	6	7	8	9
10	11	12	13	14	15	16
17	18	19	20	21	22	23
24/31	25	26	27	28	29	30

NOVEMBER

S	M	D	M	D	F	S
				1	2	3
4	5	6	7	8	9	10
11	12	13	14	15	16	17
18	19	20	21	22	23	24
25	26	27	28	29	30	

MAGGIO

D	L	M	M	G	V	S
			1	2	3	4
5	6	7	8	9	10	11
12	13	14	15	16	17	18
19	20	21	22	23	24	25
26	27	28	29	30	31	

MARZO

D	L	M	M	G	V	S
1	2	3	4	5	6	7
8	9	10	11	12	13	14
15	16	17	18	19	20	21
22	23	24	25	26	27	28
29	30	31				

DICEMBRE

D	L	M	M	G	V	S
		1	2	3	4	5
6	7	8	9	10	11	12
13	14	15	16	17	18	19
20	21	22	23	24	25	26
27	28	29	30	31		

The '70s

aprile 1974 · PIAGGIO

dicembre 1974 · PIAGGIO

gennaio 1974 · PIAGGIO

NOVEMBER 1970

S	M	T	W	T	F	S	S	M	T	W	T	F	S
1	2	3	4	5	6	7	22	23	24	25	26	27	28
8	9	10	11	12	13	14	29	30					
15	16	17	18	19	20	21							

PIAGGIO

The '80s

The '90s

PIAGGIO

April

1 2 3 4 5 6 7 8 9 10 11 12 13 14 15 16 17 18 19 20 21 22 23 24 25 26 27 28 29 30
wed thu fri sat sun mon tue wed thu fri sat sun mon tue wed thu fri sat sun mon tue wed thu fri sat sun mon tue wed thu

The Piaggio Calendar

The 2000s

Part four

COMMUNICATION

The Vespa and the Arts

The Vespa, film and television

There are films from the Fifties and Sixties in which the Vespa continuously appears in the typical urban settings of the period. There are, however, also films in which the Vespa plays roles almost as important as those of the stars. The celebrated *Roman Holiday* (directed by William Wyler), with Gregory Peck and Audrey Hepburn buzzing round Rome on a Vespa is a classic example. Other films in which the Vespa makes a significant appearance include *Poveri ma Belli, Bellezze in Bicicletta, La Notte Brava, Matrimonio all'Italiana, Le Ragazze di Piazza di Spagna, Peccato che sia una Canaglia, Un Amore a Roma, La Bella di Lodi* and *Mimì Mettallurgico*. In the film *Quadrophenia* by the rock group The Who, the singer Sting, making his film debut, rode a beautiful GS. In Federico Fellini's masterpiece *La Dolce Vita*, Marcello Mastroiani shows off Rome to Anita Ekberg aboard a Vespa. In *American Graffiti*, made in 1970, one of the protagonists arrives at the drive-in aboard his Vespa. In more recent times, Nanni Moretti toured Rome on a Vespa 150 in his *Caro Diario* from 1993.

In 1996 a video was made for use in television advertisements but it was never broadcast. In 2002 a Vespa ET4 instead appeared in the TV ad for the Fanta soft drink and, above all, received important awards for the "Aperitif" TV campaign.

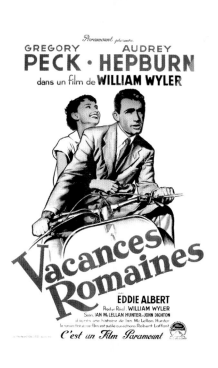

The Vespa and the Arts

Carlo Dapporto e la nuova Vespa 150

The Vespa in books, music and painting

It was not just film that underlined the fame achieved by the Vespa. Its popularity may also be gauged by citations in pop songs and even in books, many of which even had the name Vespa in the title.

Among the most important books are *Taccuino della Vespa* (Orio Vergani), *Vespina e le Streghe* (Silvio Ducati), *Storia di una Vespa Gigante e di una Vespa che Potrebbe Essere Grande Ancora* (Aldo Manos), *Convalescenza al Mare* (Luigi Brioschi). In France there was *Ma Vespa Ma Femme et Moi* (Daniel Sauvage), while Odette Ferry's *Vacances Romaines* was the basis for the celebrated film. The book by John Steinbeck, *The Short Reign of Pippin IV*, had a Vespa on the cover. The German writer, Peter Roos, described his experience touring Italy on a Vespa in *Vespa Stracciatella*. Also worthy of mention is the comic strip *Le Avventure di Pasqualino* drawn by Jacovitti and published in the early Seventies in the *Corriere dei Piccoli*.

There is then a body of travel literature, with numerous books by authors on their return from their adventures. These include, *In Vespa da Milano a Tokyo* by Roberto Patrignani (1964), *La Via delle Indie in Vespa* by Giorgio Càeran (1977) and *In Vespa Oltre l'Orizzonte* by *Giorgio Bettinelli* (1998).

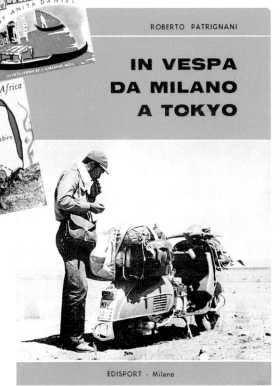

256

The Vespa and the Arts

this is mod

THE CIRCLES, THE KILLERMETERS, THE AMBER SQUAD, THE DEADBEATS, THE LETTERS, THE ODDS, THE PURPLE HEARTS, LONG TALL SHORTY, THE CIGARETTES, SMALL WORLD, THE NIPS, THE ACCIDENTS, SEMA 4, THE UNTOUCHABLES UK, THE SCENE, THE RAGE, THE SUSSED

20 MOD CLASSICS IN TRUE "MODOPHONIC" SOUND

at play with THE PLAYMATES

ORIGINAL MOTION PICTURE SOUND TRACK ALBUM

JEAN NEGULESCO'S

Jessica

MAURICE CHEVALIER
·
ANGIE DICKINSON
·
NOËL-NOEL

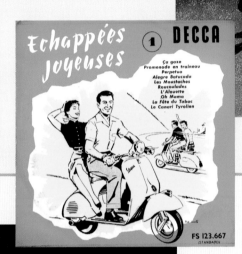

Echappées joyeuses

DECCA 1

Ça gaze
Promenade en traineau
Perpetua
Alegre Batucada
Les Moustaches
Roucoulades
L'Alouette
Oh Mama
La Fête du Tabac
Le Canari Tyrolien

FS 123.667
(STANDARD)

SIC FOR THE
NSATIONAL

The Futuramic Sounds of DON ELLIOTT AND HIS ORCHESTRA
5 TIME "DOWN BEAT" AWARD WINNER

ENZO JANNACCI
e allora... concerto

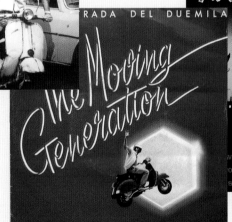

Bonnie Bianco e Pierre C...
S...

DALLA COLONNA SONORA ORIGINALE
DEL FILM

CENERENTOLA
80

ZBKT 7359

RADA DEL DUEMILA

The Moving Generation

THE RED LINES

SONGS FROM THE ORIGINAL MOTION PICTURE

Absolute Beginners
The Musical

DAVID BOWIE   JERRY DAMMERS   RAY DAVIES
ONDER featuring PATSY KENSIT   GIL EVANS   SLIM GAILLARD
SADE   STYLE COUNCIL   WORKING WEEK

The Vespa and the Arts

The Vespa literature also features the books published by Piaggio itself to celebrate particular occasions or events. A first volume appeared in 1956 to mark the scooter's 10th anniversary. The second volume came out in 1959 and celebrated the first 75 years of the Piaggio company. The was another book in 1979 for the 25th anniversary of the Vespa, while a splendid volume of images by the photographer Tam Fagiuoli with texts by Luca Goldoni was published in 1981. 1994 instead saw the appearance of Tommaso Fanfani's *Una Leggenda Verso il Futuro* on the occasion of Piaggio's 110th anniversary.

A waltz named after the Vespa and written by Tienno Pattacini was broadcast on Italian radio as early as 1948. Other waltzes followed in 1949: *La Vespa* (Antola-Fiorita) and *Via con la Vespa* (Somalvico-Carenzio). The Vespa also appeared on numerous record sleeves including, *An Actor's Holiday* (Theodore Bikel), *Side by Side* (Delta Rhythm Boys), *Basie Rides Again* (Bill Basie), *A Little Travelin' Music* (Susan Barett), *At Play With the Playmates* (Playmates), *Music for the Sensational Sixties* (Don Elliott).

In 1960, the Piaggio Magazine reproduced a painting by Renato Guttuso that depicted a couple (the woman riding side-saddle) seen from behind as they ride away on a Vespa.

The Vespa decorated by Salvador Dalí

Salvador Dalí painted in Surrealist fashion directly on the frame of the scooter belonging to two Spanish students who visited him at Cadaquez on their way from Madrid to Athens. This Vespa was to feature in "The Art of the Motorcycle" at the Guggenheim Museum in Bilbao in 2000, an exhibition with the century's most significant motorcycles.

The two students were Santiago Guillen

and Antonio Veciana. Their Vespa was a 150 built in Spain by Moto Vespa under license from Piaggio. The whole trip was completed with the bodywork decorated by the celebrated artist. The two students had visited Dalí immediately after leaving Madrid, heading for his residence at Port Ligat and it was here that the Vespa 150 was embellished with artistic brushstrokes on the side-panels and the monocoque beneath the saddle. They started on the 25th of July 1962 aiming to complete a round-the-world trip in 80 days, matching Phileas Fogg's feat in the Jules Verne novel. The journey was made by land as far as India, then by plane from Calcutta to San Francisco. Having crossed the USA from coast to coast, the Vespa was flown to London and re-entered Madrid on the 12th of October, exactly 79 days after setting out. They covered 18,950 km with no mechanical problems of note. This journey is described in the book *En 79 Dias, Vuelta al Mundo in Vespa*, published by Doncel with a preface by Dalí himself.

The Vespa and the Arts

Part five

SPORT AND TOURING

The Vespa and Racing

The Vespa and Racing

The Vespa was being taken to the tracks almost as soon as it was born. In the April of 1947, just a year after it first went on sale, Carlo Masciocchi entered his Vespa in the Gentleman Moto Club of Milan's Primi Passi event. This was a regularity trial held in the valleys above Bergamo and despite the limitations of the Vespa's small engine and a number of falls, the rider celebrated second place at the finish.

The potential of this type of event encouraged Piaggio to create a works team in which the tester Dino Mazzoncini played a leading role. The Vespa triumphed in numerous events, despite the fact that its technical characteristics made it better suited to city streets than the race track or off-road venues. Among its many victories were those in the Circuit of Florence and the Lakes Trophy in 1948 and in the Circuit of Naples and the Vicenza-Monte Gallio ski and motorbike event in 1949. That same year, Vespa finished second in the gruelling Industry Trophy that brought together three events: the Southern Shield, the 24 Hours and the Mille Miglia. In the first seven Vespas out of seven reached the finish with no penalty points. In the 24 Hours the scooters achieved similar placings, while in the Mille Miglia the seven Vespas once

The Vespa and Racing

again all finished without incurring any penalties. This was a remarkable overall result given that 500 cc motorbikes were also entered.

However, Piaggio's greatest sporting satisfaction came in the Varese International Six Days event in 1951. Of the 218 motorcycles entered for this extremely demanding regularity trial, just 89 finished without incurring penalties. Among these were no less than nine of the ten Vespas that started. 1951 also saw the introduction of single-marque championships that featured such challenging events as the 1000 km. The success of the championship led to it being repeated in 1952, while the Vespa Three Seas Tour was organized in 1953.

Competitive sporting activities were also organized outside Italy: the European Championship was staged in England in 1960, in Germany in 1961, in Belgium in 1962 and in France in 1964.

Gymkhanas were organized in numerous Italian piazzas and watched by thousands of spectators: during the Fifties and Sixties racing was the most important form of advertising.

The Vespa and Racing

The Vespa and Racing

The Vespa and record-breaking

With sporting events proving to be increasingly popular, Piaggio also decided to commit itself to breaking speed records. The Vespa's great rival, the Innocenti-built Lambretta, opened hostilities in 1949 with the conquest of 13 records on the Rome-Ostia autostrada and 36 at the French Monthléry racing circuit.

A prototype was built at Pontedera that retained links with the production model even though it was fitted with fully streamlined bodywork. The project was led by the engineers Carlo Carbonero and Vittorio Casini. This Vespa lapped Monthléry in the hands of the riders Mazzoncini, Spadoni and Castiglioni on the 6th of April 1950 and despite strong winds affecting the sessions conquered 17 records.

Piaggio's most significant triumph came in 1951: the breaking of the flying kilometre record, a feat that had enormous publicity value. Vittorio Casini was again responsible for the project, this time flanked by Corradino D'Ascanio himself.

A highly aerodynamic siluro or torpedo-shaped prototype was developed that had virtually nothing in common with the standard Vespa apart from the small-diameter wheels. The engine remained veiled in secrecy for many years. At the time the company merely

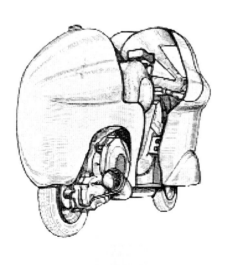

Montlhéry, 6th April 1950

50 km	average kph 134.203
50 miles	134.573
100 km	134.733
100 miles	127.777
500 km	123.463
500 miles	123.919
1000 km	124.306
1 hour	134.054
2 hours	130.794
3 hours	125.713
4 hours	123.376
5 hours	124.065
6 hours	124.636
7 hours	124.056
8 hours	124.274
9 hours	123.434

The Vespa and Racing

said that it was a single-cylinder, two-stroke unit with a "dual cylinder". In reality it was a true twin, with opposing cylinders. It was fed with a mixture of alcohol and oil by two carburettors and cooled by water. In effect, two siluri or torpedoes were constructed, a prototype and the record attempt version. This last differed with respect to the prototype in that it had doors (that acted as airbrakes) and a small spoiler in front of the minuscule windscreen.

Ridden by Dino Mazzoncini, on the 9th of February 1951 the torpedo set a new outright record of no less than 171.102 kph (the average of two runs at 174.418 and 169.910 kph) on the Rome-Ostia autostrada. The result was obtained thanks in part to the studies conducted by Marco Nuti, the head of Piaggio's Technical Innovations department. His engine produced a maximum power output of 21 hp at 9500 rpm, a highly respectable figure and obviously a great advance for a Vespa. Mazzoncini put in a superb performance, especially considering that the road surface was by no means as smooth as that of a racing circuit but full of irregularities (for the record, the measured distance was between the 10th and 11th kilometre posts). At the halfway point there was actually a hump in the asphalt that launched the vehicle into the air for a number of metres.

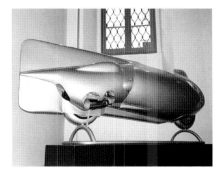

NOTIZIARIO DEL

Vespista

RASSEGNA DI TURISMO, SPORT E TECNICA
A CURA DEL GRUPPO VESPISTI ROMANI

| NUMERO UNICO | DIREZIONE E REDAZIONE
ROMA - VIA LUCREZIO CARO N. 12ª - ROMA | FEBBRAIO 1951 |

VESPA + MAZONCINI = 171 Km.h

A 174 Km. orari verso la vittoria

The Vespa and acrobatics

The Piaggio acrobatics team represents a fascinating chapter in the history of the Vespa. Founded in 1955, it was largely composed of the firm's test riders. Each year, these professional Vespisti covered hundreds of thousands of kilometres in all weathers while developing the various models, but their riding abilities were such that a select team was created within the company. Many of the members participated individually in the various organized events (such as the 1000 kilometres), but Piaggio was also happy for them to ride as team to demonstrate their abilities and the reliability of the Vespa.

Among their various turns, the most spectacular were those in which eight riders balanced on just one Vespa (or five facing backwards) or those in which they rode a Vespa and sidecar with the sidecar's wheel hanging in the air. The team also perfected a series of jumps of a number of metres; launching their Vespas from a ramp over seven barrels. These displays were staged in Italy and abroad, especially in the Far East (India and China) and South America (Brazil, Colombia) and the team continued to perform through to the end of the 1960s.

The Vespa
and endurance events

Although it was created above all as an urban vehicle, the Vespa proved to have rare qualities of reliability and robustness that made it the favourite means of transport for numerous adventurers who covered great distances on their scooters.

The first to set out on one of these memorable expeditions was the well-known journalist and rider Roberto Patrignani who crossed Asia solo in 1964 with his Vespa 150. He in fact travelled from Italy to Japan to hand over the trophy offered by the Vespa Club of Europe to the International Olympic Committee. The 13,000 km trip lasted three months and a report on his adventure was published by Patrignani in his book *In Vespa da Milano a Tokyo*. Another Vespista-explorer was Giancarlo Nuzzo who, in less than six years, traversed 47 nations and covered over 100,000 miles with his trusty GTR from 1976. Also worthy of mention is Giorgio Càeran's trip with his 200 Rally from Italy to Nepal in 1977, covering 20,000 kilometres in two months.

The Vespista to have undertaken the longest trips is Giorgio Bettinelli who has ridden his scooter to all four corners of the globe and published a richly illustrated account entitled *In Vespa oltre l'orizzonte, 110,000 kms across 60 countriwes*.

Bettinelli's trips are veritable expeditions. In 1992-93 he travelled from

Left, Antonio Corona with its Vespa Rally 200 on the way of Luxor, Egypt (1980). Below, Roberto *Patrignani and the Vespa 150 at the Olympic Games held in Tokyo in 1964.*

L'eco dell'impresa

The Vespa and Racing

Rome to Saigon (24 thousand km, 18 countries, 7 months). In 1994-95 from Alaska to Tierra del Fuego (36 thousand km, 18 countries, 9 months). In 1995-96 from Melbourne, Australia to Cape Town, South Africa (52 thousand km, 23 countries, 1 year). In 1997-2001 from Chile to Australia (144 thousand km, 90 countries, 3 years). His travel stories can also be found in the book *Brum Brum, 254.000 chilometri in Vespa*. Remarkable trips have also been completed by non-Italian Vespisti: in 1953, Pierre Delliere rode from Vietnam to Paris, covering 16 thousand km in 51 days. The same route was also taken by René Mourier in 1956, 17 thousand km in 44 days. In 1959, Georges Monneret went from Paris to the Sahara desert with his 150. James Owen instead crossed the Americas, from the United States to Tierra del Fuego. Soren Nielsen drove his Vespa to Greenland. The Englishwoman Betty Warral rode from London to Australia, while the Australian Geoff Dean completed a round-the-world trip. In 1980, four Frenchmen entered their Vespa 200 Rallies in the Paris-Dakar. But the story does not end here: there are those who have gone to sea and taken to the skies with their Vespas.

In 1952, the Frenchman Monneret linked the rear wheel of his Vespa to a propeller via rollers and rode his catamaran scooter across the English Channel from Calais to Dove in 5 hours 30'.

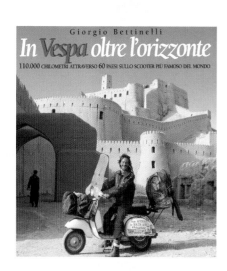

The Vespa and Racing

A surprise:

the PX Paris-Dakar

Emerging unexpectedly from the Pontedera "cellars" for a brief appearance is the legendary PX designed and built to participate in the gruelling Paris-Dakar.

The ultimate off-road marathon has seen many of the leading international motorcycling marques participate with works teams. All the vehicles venturing into the desert have been specially prepared to tackle the punishing course that traverses the Sahara before reaching Senegal.

In 1980, the Piaggio's French outpost asked Pontedera to create PX series with enduro characteristics such as knobbly tyres and a larger fuel tank (20 litres!). The PX 200 was selected for its greater power output, while the modifications included an air filter in front of the saddle and an undershield protecting the engine from damage. Four riders started from Paris and courageously tackled dunes that would have intimidated vehicles far better suited to this kind of event. Just one PX failed to finish after its steering tube broke. The other three covered 9000 km (6000 on tracks) to reach Dakar, an absolutely exceptional feat.

Part six

THE VESPA CLUB

A successful partnership

In Italy and around the world

Piaggio was not slow to recognize the promotional value of the coordination of the Vespa clubs that had been formed spontaneously ever since the scooter went on sale. The framework was established by Renato Tassinari. A former sub-editor at the *Gazzetta dello Sport* and subsequently at the *Corriere dello Sport*, Tassinari was the right man in the right place. In 1948, he was asked to organize the Piaggio stand at the Milan trade fair. Enthusiastic and long-sighted coordinator that he was, Tassinari invented the "silver swarm" and brought together under his direction 2000 Vespisti from all over Italy.

The success of this initiative encouraged Piaggio to organize the clubs with ever greater efficiency. On the 23rd of October 1949, the Vespa Club d'Italia was officially born with the organization of the first National Conference at Viareggio. The president was Renato Tassinari. On the 9th of December 1951, delegates from the various Italian Vespa clubs attended the conference in Rome where the new publication *Vespa Club Italia* was presented. Distributed to all members, the periodical kept them informed about the club's various activities. By the end of 1959, the year the Vespa Club d'Italia celebrated its 10th anniversary at Viareggio,

A successful partnership

there were no less than 220 Italian clubs with over 50,000 members. The same city also saw the club celebrate its 20th anniversary in 1969, 30th in 1979 and 40th in 1989…

In 1973 the president of the Vespa Club d'Italia was Manlio Riva, succeeded in 1984 by Roberto Leardi.

An important initiative, the birth of the Historical Register, took place within the ambit of the Legnago conference in the December of 1980. The first curator was Mario Carini, a leading figure in the history of the Vespa in Italy. In 1984, he was succeeded by Luigi Frisinghelli. The aim of the register is that of preserving the historical models and conserving those of particular interest to collectors. In 1985, the first rallies devoted to classic scooters were held at Castiglione della Pescaia (Grosseto) and Grottaferrata (Rome). 1953 saw the birth of the Vespa Club of Europe in Milan (Italy, France, Germany, Switzerland, Netherlands and Belgium). Some Vespa Clubs were born also outside Europe: in South Africa, Libya, Hong Kong and Thailand.

In 1984, Christa Solbach of Germany was nominated as President of the International Federation of International Vespa Clubs.

A successful partnership

The rallies

The first Vespa Day was staged on the 6th of May 1953, with no less than 20,000 Vespisti attending rallies in 12 different cities. The success of this initiative encouraged Piaggio to organize a second day in 1956, with 56,000 Vespisti attending in 16 cities.
Eurovespa, the event bringing together Vespisti from throughout Europe was also a great success. In 1955, at San Remo, 13 countries were represented, with the same number being present at Munich in 1956. Over 2000 Vespisti attended the EuroVespa event in Barcelona in 1957. Subsequently, events

were held in Brussels in 1958, Paris in 1959, Rome in 1960 and Salzburg in 1961.
In more recent times, EuroVespa has been held in Rome in 1981, Reggio Calabria in 1982, Austria in 1983, Verona in 1984, Barcelona in 1986, Switzerland in 1990, San Marino in 1991, Germany in 1992, Abano Terme in 1993, Spain in 1994, San Remo in 1996, Greece in 1997 and Holland in 1998.

A successful partnership

Part seven

THE PONTEDERA MUSEUM

The origins of the legend

The historical legacy

The Piaggio
Museum

Inaugurated on the 29th of March 2000, the Pontedera museum is a fundamental point of reference in the history of the Vespa. The fact that today we are able to admire this exhibition space is due largely to Giovanni Alberto Agnelli who passed away prematurely in 1997 at just 36 years of age. The Piaggio chairman from 1988, the young Agnelli was the first to propose a cultural project that would promote the company's heritage. The point of departure was the creation of the foundation in 1994 that laid the basis for the collection and cataloguing of the documentation relating to the entire Piaggio story. Heading up and coordinating the foundation since 1998 is Professor Tommaso Fanfani.

The museum was established at the company's Pontedera factory in spaces created in the former toolshop. In this way the link between the history of the Vespa and that of the Piaggio company is strengthened. The museum features not only the most important models from the Vespa line-up, but also acknowledges Piaggio's other significant achievements: from aircraft (on the forecourt) to trains. An example of the stainless steel railcar actually "enters" the museum itself. A number of radial aero engines are also on display inside.

The origins of the legend

Naturally, there are examples of racing and record-breaking Vespas, the Ape, the 400 small car and the Moscone outboard motor (with a splendid section). One particularly intriguing exhibit: the one-off prototype Vespa used in the 1967 film *Dick Smart* complete with a rotary wing. For lovers of the Gilera, there is a mezzanine floor with the most significant historical models, from the unique VT 317 from 1909 to the Paris-Dakar RC 600 from 1991. Also on display is a highly streamlined Gilera record-breaker from 1937.

Vespa production models are well represented by a series of particularly important and well displayed examples. Some are located in a large hall, others are actually mounted in three rows on the wall. The right-hand side of each of these is displayed allowing the engine to be presented and from a distance it almost seems as though you are looking at a magnificent series of models enclosed in their boxes. Only they are, of course, life-size! A visit to the museum is a fascinating and enthralling experience for all Vespa enthusiasts.

The origins of the legend

The "Antonella Bechi Piaggio" Historical Archive

The Historical Archive is located within the museum and boasts a wealth of documents, drawings, sketches and advertising material. The majority of the over 150,000 documents are from the offices of the Pontedera and Genoa factories. The original nucleus is constituted by the Lanzara Archive, named after the engineer Francesco Lanzara, the director of the factories between 1940 and 1979. Successively the following acquisitions were added: the Legal Documents Archive (foundation deeds and assembly minutes), the General Management Archive (account books and administrative deeds), the Commercial Management Archive (brochures and press reviews), the Iconographical Archive (photographs and films), the Production and Design Archive (research and technical manuals), the Personnel Archive (organization and social activities), the S.A.R.P.I. Archive (marketing between 1948 and 1961) and the Gilera Archive (documentation from Arcore). An appropriate acknowledgement for the historical resource containing all the most important documentation regarding the Vespa.

The origins of the legend

The origins of the legend

The origins of the legend

The origins of the legend

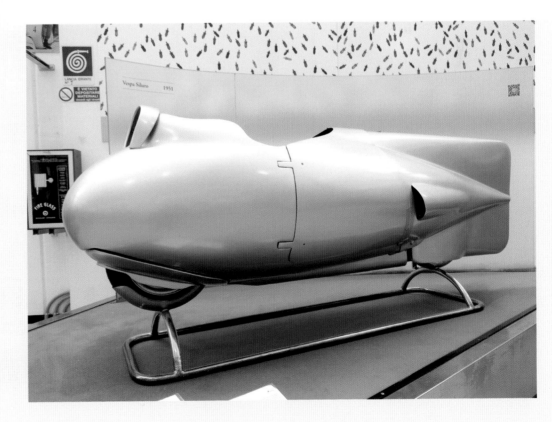

The origins of the legend

The origins of the legend

Part eight

VESPA COLLECTING

Culture and Passion

Culture and Passion

The universe comprising everything orbiting around the Vespa is boundless and extremely varied. While collecting of the various historic models may be taken for granted, it might instead come as surprise to learn of the number of product categories in which the Vespa name appears, sufficient to arouse the desire for possession of countless enthusiasts.

The initial extension of the Vespa universe came with the accessories market. In the scooter's period of greatest commercial success – the Fifties – few could resist the temptation to embellish their Vespa, drawing on a vast range of extras offered by various companies in the sector. Not to speak of those all but essential accessories such as the speedometer/milometer.

Then came the vast toy sector that saw the Vespa being reproduced to scale and fitted with pedals to satisfy the dreams of the youngest fans. A gift that many Vespa-riding fathers were only too willing to put under the Christmas tree or purchase for their child's birthday.

It was not only scale versions of the Vespa, there were also board games such as the remarkable "Vespa World Tour", which even attracted those adults quite happy to travel by Vespa from

Culture and Passion

the comfort of their own home on even the coldest and wettest of days.

It comes as no surprise to see the passion for the Vespa in modelling circles. A sector that has always enjoyed great popularity among car, bike and scooter enthusiasts who can thereby indulge their passions without investing a fortune in full-size examples. Not to mention the fact that a display case is sufficient to contain a fine collection.

However, the Vespa fans go much further and place many objects in their display cases such as badges and medals. Bits and bobs? No, a wealth of objects actually. Going back to the golden years, there was not a Vespa rally that did not feel the need to make metal ornaments commemorating the event.

For the collector that has to have everything, Owners Handbooks can hardly be ignored. Perhaps even for models that are not in their garage but which might complete a series. Can we go even further? Of course; there are also the workshop manuals in which the drawings of the individual components and the "exploded" diagrams of the assemblies get the engineering enthusiasts panting.

Culture and Passion

Then there are the rare and sought after cups and statuettes created for the sporting events. A must for many enthusiasts who are well aware of the importance of the competitive events featuring the Vespa. Events such the "Giro dei Tre Mari", or the "1000 Km Vespistica still set hearts beating many years later.

Then there is a whole series of objects that range from ties to watches, passing by way of those unthinkable today such as ashtrays and cigarette lighters.

The list of products goes on and we have to consider the whole two-dimensional world which ranges from stamps to postcards. These last, in particular, could cover entire walls as so many have been produced over the years. Those with plenty of space might opt for the giant of the printed genre, the original film posters. There are of course filing cabinets for these collectibles, but decorating a wall with original posters is something else and for the film and Vespa buffs a unique opportunity to put their passions on display.

An intermediate path, but one that is particularly popular, is that of calendars. In part because from the outset, Piaggio has always relied on beautiful girls, with a graphic style that has

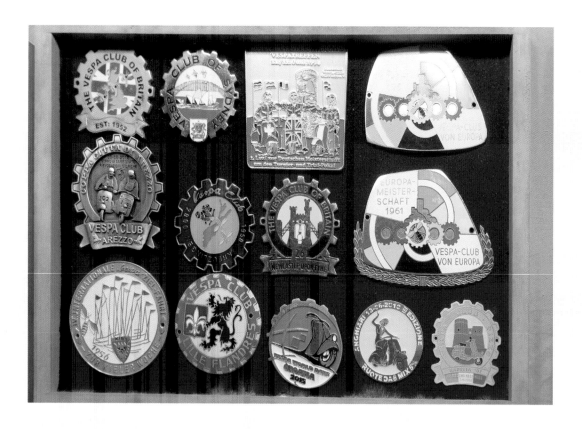

Culture and Passion

evolved over the years: from the drawings of the early years to photographs, from the less audacious to the more daring poses, always keeping pace with the times and occasionally anticipating fashions. The calendar has always appealed to everyone, in part because the models were recruited from the world of show business and were therefore already well known and beautifully photographed.

In terms of printed matter, mention also has to be made of the in-house "Rivista Piaggio", which for many years was a source of endless news items and fine illustrations, maintaining close bonds between Mamma-Piaggio and the enthusiastic Vespisti.

Culture and Passion

Original accessories

The question of original accessories was of particular importance in the Vespa world. At the time, not everyone would fit them to their Vespa, in part due to what in certain cases was their significant cost. The Veglia-Borletti speedometer/milometer for example, was a universal object of desire, but few could afford to make the purchase. Many years later, the dilemma has returned, this time for those intent on a restoration project: leave the instrument as it is, perhaps non-functioning, or replace it with one that works perfectly? Once again, the difference comes down to a question of cost. With regard to availability, there are various shows and fairs, but prices are frequently sky high, at times exceeding even 500 Euros. You might see €1000 being asked for one of the legendary Rolles. It is not just the restorers who are on the look-out for speedometers. There are also collectors who, perhaps to complete a particular collection or due to a lack of space, actually focus on accessories. The desirable items are much more numerous than you might think; just flick through the Fabbri catalogue (which itself costs a few hundred Euros). The offer ranges from metal profiles to protect the front mudguard to crash bars for the side covers,

Culture and Passion

from reflectors to the inevitable tax disc holder, from mechanical anti-theft devices to indicators. And for the scooterist who has everything there is even a little aeroplane to be fitted to the tip of the mudguard.

Toys

You can own a Vespa even before your eagerly awaited 14th birthday (the age at which 50 cc mopeds and scooters may be ridden on the roads in Italy). In reality, you can be much younger, just as long as you do not insist on an engine under the frame and are happy pedalling... The fortunate children of the 1950s who received a mini-Vespa on their birthdays or for Christmas could hardly have been happier: this was the kind of gift dreams were made of. Even today, when they find a toy Vespa the collectors have the same reaction. However, then they have to open their wallets and that is when things start to become painful... The prices being asked frequently exceed €1000, especially for the metal models made in the Fifties. They tend to come down only for the more modern versions, like those produced in the Seventies but in plastic materials. You can go even lower in terms of price, but then you will have to settle

Culture and Passion

for the models made in Russia in the Eighties, which it safe to say are hardly the most sought after. In the golden age, various models were produced in Italy and there were also examples from France and Germany. On the Italian scene, of particular note were the models from Lupetta (with the centrally mounted spare wheel) and Kinderbaby (which reprised the Fifties look). In France, the models made by Pierre Guy caught the eye, while in Germany the Ferbedo featured perfectly a functioning horn and indicators. The only problem with a collection of this kind is the space that it occupies: these are hardly scale models to be displayed on a shelf.

**The Vespa
World Tour**

There is more to life than Monopoly. For dyed-in-the-wool Vespisti the most important board game focuses on the Vespa and takes the form of an adventurous Tour of the World. Fair warning before you throw yourselves into the hunt for the game at the next sale or fiar: the prices asked frequently exceed €500. Which says much about the scarcity of supply and the extent of demand. However, these prices are justified when you find a

Culture and Passion

mint game in the original box. Naturally with the pieces all present and correct. In any case, the game itself, made in the 1950s, is fantastic. There were probably many fathers at the time who bought it for their children so they could play it themselves. It featured lavish use of illustrations colour and the Vespa script appeared everywhere, confirming the association with the "real" vehicle. Naturally, the miniature Vespa is the true protagonist of the game: for the record there are actually six, one for each of the players attempting to complete the World Tour. It's a game based on throwing dice, with chance being part of the fun. As you may imagine, victory goes to player who reaches the destination first, but the task is anything but easy. As happens in the real world, rules have to be respected (keeping to the right for example), caution is required (avoiding icy roads) and you have to careful to avoid running out of fuel. The game was also popular with French children (and their fathers), who even had a version with a convenient carrying case in place of the usual cardboard box.

Culture and Passion

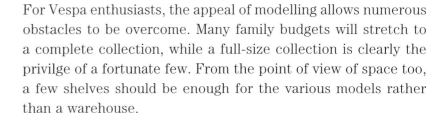

Scale models

For Vespa enthusiasts, the appeal of modelling allows numerous obstacles to be overcome. Many family budgets will stretch to a complete collection, while a full-size collection is clearly the privilge of a fortunate few. From the point of view of space too, a few shelves should be enough for the various models rather than a warehouse.

Where should you begin? With the oldest models of course, even though these are the most expensive. However, they first appeared immediately after the launch of the Vespa and went on sale before the end of the 1940s. Among the most sought after pieces are the wonderful models by Ferrari Siro of Casalpusterlengo. In the Fifties, the INGAP (Industria Nazionale Giocattoli Automatici Padova) brand became famous for its vast and highly accuate range spanning various genres. With regard to the section devoted to the Vespa, the models even featured a figure in the saddle and sidecar versions. Naturally, there have also been numerous models produced outside Italy. In France, of particular note are those by Hotte St Nicolas, Solido and BS Miniatur. In Spain there are JD, Ves Bretta and Payaso. In Denmark, Tekno stands out. And Germany? Nothing

Culture and Passion

to report, modelling there has for some reason always focused on the Lambretta. In contrast, there are plenty of fine examples of Vespa models from distant lands such as those by Bandai in Japan and Lincoln in Hong Kong.

Badges
and medals

It truly is difficult to imagine the vastness of the range of badges and medals that have been produced over the decades. Every Vespa club worthy of the name has an emblem for its personal use and given that there are hundreds of clubs throughout Italy and around the world, the numbers soon mount up. For the record, the total is more than 1,500, which equates to an ocean of badges and pins. Just think, there are four different plaques for the Vespa Club Europa alone and there is hardly a collector who does not dream of finding all four. If the number appears high it is because, especially in the 1950s, not a weekend would pass without a dedicated rally or show being organized, not to mention the gymkhanas. And any event without its own dedicated emblem would have would hardly have been worthy of consideration. Where were these plaques mounted? Gener-

Culture and Passion

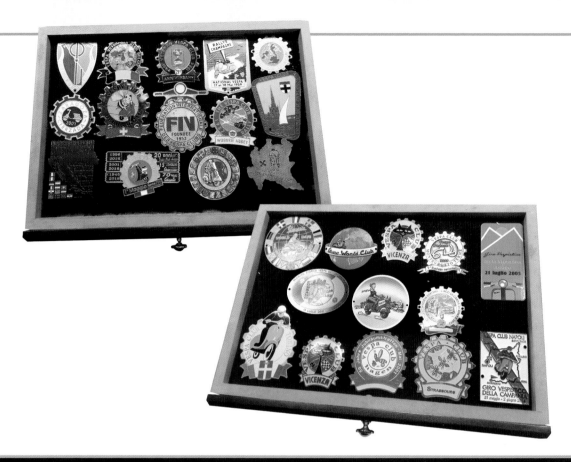

Culture and Passion

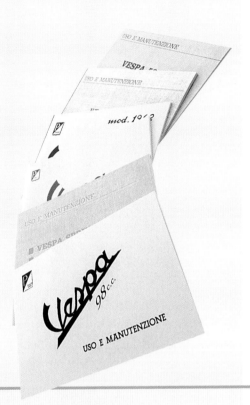

ally on the leg shield, mercilessly drilled (a sacrilege today) in order to display the coveted badge. As for the illustrated logo, the only limit was that of the imagination, although the graphic element of a toothed cog wheel was usually included as it was the symbol of the Vespa Club itself. Among the most sought after badges are those made for the most prestigious competitive events, such as the celebrated Giro dei Tre Mari or the 1000 Km. Those celebrating the most important rallies such as the famous Eurovespa are also cult objects.

Handbooks and workshop manuals

How much might an Owner's Handbook be worth? When the scooter was first purchased, very little. Most owners would stash them under the saddle and never think about them again. Only to flounder in the dark every time they had to check the tyre pressures. It might be thought that with the passing of the years, the value of these booklets would have become derisory. Quite the contrary: try attending a sale or fair and see how just how valuable the manuals are now... try asking the price! In this case too, the law of supply and demand comes into play

Culture and Passion

and for the sought-after Vespas (such as the GS) the prices rise steeply. Along with the Owner's Handbooks there are also the Workshop Manuals, usually destined exclusively for those dealers that also offered maintenance services. Getting hold of one of these means joining a restricted circle of particularly keen-eyed collectors. There are also other sought-after bits of paper such as the registration documents that have always been indispensable if the machine was to be ridden on the road or bought and sold. Over the years, many of these documents have been lost and as if by magic turn up on the stalls at the fairs. All relics which the collectors pick up to enrich their own collections, but are not necessarily associated with a roadworthy Vespa. There are those who have entire albums and stories to tell about each document. If only those papers could talk!

Novelties

While every Vespa rally and event, even the most modest, had their own badges, it is not hard to imagine the wealth of cups, plaques and medals that were produced for the various sporting occasions and to celebrate the major events. Among the

Culture and Passion

most sought-after items for collectors are the sculptures with reproduction Vespas, in particular the one dedicated to the millionth example which features a little plinth with the caption "Pontedera, 2-4-1956". Also of value is the official coin with the Piaggio badge, a true collector's item. Then there are numerous commemorative plaques and Touring Trophies. The most valuable pieces are those in solid bronze, which in certain cases may weigh a number of kilos. The Giro dei Tre Mari cup is particularly sought after, in part because its shape recalls that of the historic Mille Miglia car race.

They might not be Ming vases, but for many collectors they are all but priceless: statuettes in ceramic, usually sculpted with a figure (almost always female) at the controls of the Vespa. In some cases there is also a passenger. Some pieces reproduce a static scene, while others succeed in rendering the idea of movement, perhaps with skirts and hair flowing in the wind. As these are delicate, fragile objects, the prices can be rather high.

Culture and Passion

Those objects of a certain value carrying the Piaggio logo are particularly coveted. Among them are watches and clocks that are destined to remain a dream for many collectors given their rarity and value.

There are valuable table models, but also wristwatches, prestigious objects in their own right that acquire a much greater value when they carry the Pontedera logo. There are, however, alternative that are perhaps not quite so prestigious but still significant. The world of smokers, for example (probably outlawed today!) is particularly rich in objects that are much more affordable than the clocks and watches and range from ashtrays to match boxes. The prices rise with lighters, with the most sought after being the Zippo model with the engraved drawing of the Vespa by Raymond Savignac. Then there are ties complete with tie clip for a touch of elegance and even a perfume stick for "refreshment on the move", aboard a Vespa of course, as shown in the him and her illustrations with their respective scooters.

Culture and Passion

Postcards

If you wanted to collect them all you could fill entire albums and occupy numerous shelves. The quantity of postcards featuring the Vespa is endless; every self-respecting collector accumulates them avidly and some of them are stunning. The theme was developed above all in the Fifties and Sixties, when drawings ruled and the quality of the printing was frequently superb. One name above all: Cecami, a publishing company specialising in this kind of product. If anyone is asking why these postcards were never seen in shops and tobacconists, the answer is simple: they were never commercialised. In fact they were sent out by Mamma Piaggio to the various dealers, a custom that was very common in Italy and other countries such as France, Great Britain, Spain and Germany. An elegant means of sending news to the sales network. Moreover, the Vespa Clubs would also frequently use postcards to communicate changes of address or the dates of their rallies. How can you resist?

Culture and Passion

Punti di vista...

L'impiego più pratico

Lascia fare alle curve

Culture and Passion

"Federico, the pizza-man"

Culture and Passion

Collecting and postage stamps have always formed a natural pairing and it is hardly surprising that the two worlds are linked by the Vespa as a subject. A stamp that is coveted by all collectors is the one issued on the 28th of April 1956: at date which confirmed Vespisti will know because of the celebrations for the millionth Vespa. For the record, this was actually a letter seal as it did not carry a monetary value, but it can nevertheless be grouped with the true stamps. It has to be said that see the number of different Vespa models represented creates a certain effect. Another important piece is the stamp celebrating the first 50 years of the Vespa (value 750 lire), issued in 1996: all yellow because it reprised the celebrated poster by Raymond Savignac, despite being printed in three million examples, it is fairly rare today. Perhaps there is no need for this warning except for those who are new to the world of stamps: you should always use tweezers, never pick up a stamp with your fingers as if it were any old piece of paper, otherwise you risk damage and a consequent drop in value. There are of course special albums with convenient pockets.

Culture and Passion

Culture and Passion

Film posters

Here we are getting into a very unusual niche area due to the size of this particular object of desire. Real posters rather than flyers, are as big as sheets and couple will cover the walls of a garage. You can always keep them in flat in files where they can be leafed through like the pages of a book, but in this case their visual impact is severely reduced. For those fortunate enough to have sufficient space, the theme is of particular interest and for a collector who is also a film buf then the pleasure is doubled. In any case, there are numerous films that feature the Vespa which is clearly visible on the poster. Naturally, everyone knows Roman Holiday starring Audrey Hepburn and Gregory Peck, but others that are just as spectacular but less well-known include Jessica, La Ragazza Supersprint and Esame di Guida.

Culture and Passion

Calendars

Few collectibles are as close to the hearts of the enthusiasts as the Piaggio calendar. From the outset the calendars featured pretty girls and Vespas with obvious appeal that went beyond the ranks of the Vespisti and also attracted graphic design fans. Only the Pirelli calendar can compete in terms of sophistication, but it is Mamma Piaggio's product that sparks the cravings of the Vespa collectors. The calendar launched in 1951 in rather muted fashion, with just six pages for the 12 months. In recompense, the drawings by Franco Mosca were fabulous and set a trend. Six pages and drawings by Mosca again for the following 1952, 1953 and 1954 and then, from 1955, came a change that in its way was fundamental: 12 pages and photographs. For many collectors, this transformation from the "Boccasile" style [Boccasile being a well-known Italian illustrator] to the realism of photography represents a watershed and the calendars from the first four years are the most sought-after. In part because a specific theme was developed for each year, ranging from travel to sport, from local holidays to exotic locations. Over the years, numerous actresses and models appeared who were to go on to become famous figures in the world of show business: Piaggio

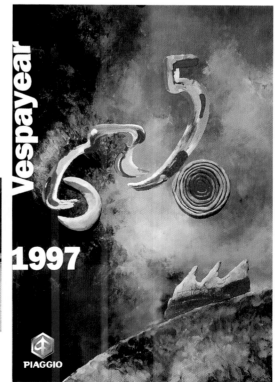

Culture and Passion

can rightly be said to have been a great talent scout! Among the many girls to feature were the sisters Alice and Ellen Kessler and Raffaella Carrà, Sylva Koshina and Angie Dickinson, Catherine Spaak and Ursula Andress, Raquel Welch and Romina Power. Chapeau!

The Piaggio magazine

The Piaggio could hardly escape the interest of the collectors, a publication with a wealth of articles and photographs that was as popular when it was published as it is fascinating today. Leafing through the volumes today the thrill of discovery is added to the enthusiasm that shone through on every page. Enthusiasm that was immediately apparent in the remarkable editorials written by Renato Tassinari, the editor of the magazine and the tireless president of the Vespa Club Italia. The Piaggio magazine was first published in 1949 and appeared in 1950, 1951 and 1952, but without a regular schedule. Things changed in 1954 (with an article by Corradino d'Ascanio appearing in the first issue): the publication appeared every two months to the delight of the many enthusiasts. The covers became ever

Culture and Passion

more sophisticated and there was a clear intent to produce a quality publication. In 1956, along with the issue every two months, a 96-page book was also published and is today eagerly sought-after by all collectors. After all, that year there were the celebrations marking the 10th anniversary of the Vespa and the millionth example produced. Further innovations came in 1957 with colour pages that made the magazine even more attractive. Then there was nothing new to report until 1963 when the magazine was published on a quarterly basis, while in 1966 this cadence was further reduced to every four months. It was clear that Piaggio's interest in the magazine was waning and in 1974 just a single issue was published. The definitive closure came in 1976, leaving many Vespisti very disappointed.

The Vespa Club newsletter

The Piaggio magazine is not the only publication to attract the interest of collectors. The printed matter dealing with the Vespa world also features the Vespa Club d'Italia's newsletter. The club had been founded as early as 1949 and its newsletter first appeared in 1952. This "Newsletter for Ital-

Culture and Passion

ian Vespisti" as the subtitle ran, featured everything that fell within the orbit of the Vespa world ranging from the infinite rallies to the races (both domestic and international) and conventions and more besides. When there was a national or European rally on the horizon, the newsletter went into overdrive with detailed articles providing comprehensive information. Not to speak of the excitement aroused by the presentation of a new Vespa model, front page news that mesant that the newsletter became a mine of information that was as important at the time as it is (perhaps even more so) now. Then there are the readers' letters that established direct links between the enthusiasts and what was going on at Mamma Piaggio. What is striking is the continuous year by year increase in the number of Italian Vespa Clubs: from 50 in 1952 to 170 in 1956. The situation stabilized in the 1960s and by the end of the decade interest had started to decline and the newsletter was discontinued in 1970.

Culture and Passion

The collector of reference: Marco Fumagalli

Marco Fumagalli (1973) of Seregno is the most important Vespa collector we know of, a reputation earned thanks to the extent and the quality of his collection. Along with possessing the widest range of models existing, Fumagalli's immense knowledge and experience has to be recognised. This derives in part from a painstakingly assembled selection of printed matter that, over the years, has been studied, classified and ordered as never before. The collection comprises not only every model to have left Pontedera, but also an immense quantity of objects associated with the Vespa world.

Q. Marco Fumagalli, why don't you introduce yourself.
I've always been a great engineering enthusiast, having grown up between home and the workshop. My family's business has always been associated with mechanical engineering, in particular the production of springs, which took place in a wing of our house. You'd cross the living room to get to the office and then through to the workshop.

Q. So your relationship with "machinery" got off to an early start...

A. *Yes, I clearly remember the thrill when as a young boy I drove my first motor vehicle, my mother's car. I was 10 years old and when we got home from school, I'd help my mother so that she didn't have to get in and out of the car to open and close the gate.*

Culture and Passion

Q. How did the Vespa collection come about?

A. *First and foremost, I've never considered the Vespa to be a motorcycle and this encouraged me to get to know it better. And the more I explored, the more incredibly interesting aspects I found. Along with the fact that over the course of the years the Vespa has become an icon of Italian industry and design. In short, something that goes far beyond the mere mechanical object.*

Q. When did you start?

A. *My first "fatal" encounter with the Vespa came in 1991, with what was a decidedly original series. It may have been pure chance, but this was a model that today, years later, is virtually unknown. It was in fact already a collectible without me knowing it. That year, Piaggio brought out a Special Edition of the 50 Special, assembling components from various earlier versions. It's still not clear why, but it was officially known as the Revival. It was this very special piece, even though I had no way of knowing at the time, that opened the door and showed me a path I'm still following.*

Q. And when did the collection as such begin to take shape?

A. *That was in 1998. Through to that point I had been satisfied with my Special, but then something clicked and I began to seek out models from the Fifties to restore. Naturally, this also involved research into the relative documentation and here a whole world opened up, the dimensions of which I could never have imagined.*

Q. So you also began accumulating printed matter.

A. *Yes, and the more I dug the more I discovered how much material I was*

Marco Fumagalli reviewing part of his fabulous collection.

Culture and Passion

missing to complete the collection. Initially I searched for all the official brochures and then moved on to the workshop manuals and mechanical drawings. Until you immerse yourself in this world, it's hard to get an idea just how much material there is around. Or rather, that there was around. Finding it after so many years is pretty demanding.

Q. And then there are the magazines, the club newsletters...

A. *The Piaggio magazine has of course become a must, both for the information it contains and for the quality and quantity of the illustrations. Over the years I've collected every issue of this magazine, including the legendary No. 1. Leafing through it after all this time what emerges is the incredible enthusiasm that permeated the*

Vespa world, above all in the 1950s. Naturally this was thanks in part to the periodical's tireless editor, Renato Tassinari. You could make a book out of his enthusiastic editorials alone.

Q. Is there anything missing from your immense collection?

A. *In terms of models, I'd have to say no. Sure, I'm missing the one-offs that you'll find in the Pontedera museum, but clearly it's right that they're exhibited on home turf. With regards to the gadgets instead, there's always something else; the Vespa is present in an infinite range of product sectors.*

Q. For example?

A. *The list is endless. It goes from scale models, to pedal scooters for toddlers, from postcards to statuettes, from*

Culture and Passion

Culture and Passion

official gadgets to the commemorative items from the rallies, from racing trophies to badges, from patches to postage stamps, from film posters to flags. And so much more; I've filled entire display cases!

Q. In any case, behind every acquisition there's always negotiation. Who knows how many sellers and collectors you've met. How many stories...

A. *In reality, things have almost always been very straightforward. There's never been a piece that I've had to work particularly hard to bring home. I've always said to the previous owners or collectors that if one day they were ready to sell I'd be there... and that is how it went on numerous occasions. Sure, it also took a whole lot of patience! And I have to say, that all the enthusiasts I've met have always kept their word; they could have tried bumping up the price by claiming others were interested, but fortunately there are still people who are as good as their word.*

Q. We're not talking just Vespa. There's room in your collection for the Ape, the Moscone...

A. *And the Ciao for that matter! Sure, the collection is not as complete as the Vespa one, but I could hardly not have a few examples of the Ape. The same goes for the Moscone outboard, which is also on display in various versions.*

Q. Among the many stories in which you feature, there one that is very special. The one in involving you and the Bonneville Salt Flats, the record-breaking location par excellence.

A. *Now that was a unique adventure! For the moment at least, although I hope to go back one day. It all came about as a bit of a joke, without taking into consideration too many technical and logistical aspects. However, as time passed and the date of the event drew closer, all our doubts or problems had been resolved and...*

off I went. With what? With a radically modified version of the Vespa.

Q. Then what?

A. *The key was having tried to make the various modifications to both the frame and the engine, without distorting the concept of the Vespa as all we enthusiasts know it. But there's a but. The regulation is very clear and defines the position of the engine with respect to the axis of the wheels of the vehicle. I believe that the Vespa is the only two-wheeled vehicle to have the engine mounted laterally! It was therefore impossible to respect this particular regulation, which meant that... no homologation for the record in our category! Still, we did have great fun and considerable satisfaction.*

Q. Who was involved in this enterprise?

A. *The team, if I can call it that, was*

The collector of reference:
Marco Fumagalli

composed of friends who participated by contributing 100% of their talents. Three Vespa models were prepared and all three competed. I personally rode two, while the other was ridden by Mauro Pascoli. Today, these three models, differing in terms of displacement and category, are found in three different places. One example is in my museum, one is in Ravenna while the other is to be found in Livorno. This last is kept by Marco Quaretta, who dealt with the technical aspects of all three.

Q. With regard to your collection, is there a time limit? Through to the Eighties perhaps. There are so many...

A. No, no! The collection continues as long as Piaggio keeps selling the Vespa! I've models from the 90s, the 2000s, 2010s, 2020s and so on. The last to be added was the 75th anniversary Primavera 125. I make my choices based on what's available on the market and my preferences at that moment.

Q. Do you have a favourite Vespa model? Or is that like asking a father about his children?

A. Well, it's difficult to say. All the models have their own personality. However, I particularly like riding the 125 from 1951, the one everybody knows from the film Roman Holiday.

Q. There must be one that is the most valuable.

A. Yes, above all others, even the 98, that would be the 125 Sei Giorni from 1953. □

Culture and Passion

Printed by Lito Terrazzi, Iolo (PO)
April 2022